The Hauxton Fossil Diggings

Bernard O'Connor

Bernard O'Connor

Researching parish history is a fascinating hobby. It's like being a detective – piecing together bits of evidence to try to find out what happened in the past. What has emerged tells not only an interesting story of the development of an extractive industry but also an account of the coprolite diggings in the Hauxton area. It also gives insight into the social, economic and religious factors that shaped local people's lives in the second half of the nineteenth century.

When I first came to this area in 1986 I read in a geological account of East Anglia that an iguanodon had been dug up in the Potton Greensand. I made it my business to find the monster. Its search revealed a fascinating industry that covered a lot more than just Hauxton. Just contacting people in the area was not enough. I have had help from numerous sources that ought to be acknowledged. The staff at the Sedgwick Earth Sciences Museum, the Cambridge Record Office, the Cambridge Collection, Cambridge University Library, the Church and Charity Commissioners in London and the Public Records Office in Kew need special thanks. I also need to acknowledge the assistance of the Masters Fellows and students of Jesus College, Queens College, St Catherine's College and Trinity College, Cambridge whose archivists were very helpful in providing access to their 19th century estate records. Mr Blackthorn-Maze of Barrington kindly donated the Barrington coprolite. The late George Rogers of Grantchester gave me many details of the First World War workings and Henry Boot and Son very kindly helped with the photographs. George Hunt, John Jennings and D.R. Hadden contributed useful facts and many others have given snippets of background information. Digging into the 19th century history of Hauxton has shed light on many people whose lives were changed by this unique industry.

Similar accounts of other parishes on the coprolite belt can be obtained from –

www.bernardoconnor.org.uk

In 1856 a new industry started in the fields on the west of the River Cam around Haslingfield, a small parish about seven miles southwest of Cambridge. In time it spread through surrounding parishes and across the river into Hauxton. It provided a very different occupation to agricultural work, that of coprolite digging, locally called "fossiling." What follows is an examination of the social, religious and economic impact this unusual industry had on this area.

Until the nineteenth century Hauxton was a small agricultural community that had not changed much since the Middle Ages. Over the first twenty years of the century its population more than doubled to 236. Medical improvements reduced infant mortality and having ten children was not unusual. By 1843 it peaked at 313 and then stabilised for a decade before declining towards the end of the century. But something happened in the second half of the century that very much brought this area into the Victorian era of industrial and economic change. Most of the villagers were engaged as agricultural labourers on the local farms on the estate or were employed as domestics or labourers in the houses of the gentry. Families like the Cantelupes and the Bendyshes lived in grand style with butlers, maids, a governess and gardeners whilst the villagers lived in small, cramped thatched cottages with a small garden for growing fruit and vegetables, keeping a pig and chickens.

Life in agricultural communities was not the quiet and peaceful rural idyll that characterised traditional images of country life. There were tremendous economic and social changes brought about in the nineteenth century. The introduction of the Enclosures after 1799 and the implementation of the new technology introduced during the "Agricultural Revolution" had a dramatic impact on rural villages. Many farm labourers became entirely dependent of the farmers for their livelihood. There were "hiring fairs"where men and women were taken on according to the decoration of their lapel.

The historian, David Ellison, referred to this period in Whaddon and commented on the "startling" social effects which resulted.

> "The repeal of the Corn Laws and the lower prices of corn for farmers had made them all try to save costs by mechanisation and reducing their labour forces. Little wonder that the first section of the Mormon church in this part of England, outside Bedford, had its first headquarters there - they encouraged and advanced money, for men to emigrate with their families across the Atlantic to a promised land - and, oddly enough, one of the appeals of their church was that almost anyone could become a priest in it. Cambridge's farm labourers had often noticed the immense gulf between themselves with their £25 to £30 a year, and the rectors with £300 - £400, comfortable rectories, and often land as well as house servants."

(Ellison, D. 'Coprolites in the Orwell area,' part of Orwell history topics; Ref. Latter Day Saints Millennial Star, passim, and Kowallis, Gay P. (1970?), 'To the Great Salt Lake from Litlington,' Bassingbourn)

As farm labourers they tended to live in tied cottages which they could easily be evicted from at the whim of the farmer or farm bailiff. Not being seen at church for the Sunday service was a dismissible offence. Afterwards they had to wait by the door of the pub until the Lord of the Manor went in. There was considerable poverty and overcrowding in crumbling "shit and stubble" or wattle and daub thatched cottages in many rural villages. New steam-powered agricultural machinery, designed to save time and labour, was introduced by farmers who were keen to profit from the increased demand for food. These machines like the steam traction engine, threshing machine, deep plough and elevator resulted in an increasing number of redundancies in farm labour. Some developed useful mechanical skills but there was widespread unrest in most rural communities. Many landless peasants were forced off the land when they lost the right to use the open fields. The loss of gleaning rights after harvest, the loss of the common for grazing animals and poultry, the denial of access to the newly fenced or walled in woodland reduced their "free" catch of rabbit, pheasant, partridge, nuts and wild fruit.

Over the first half of the century most parishes in this area experienced out-emigration as the more motivated sections of the community, mainly young adult males and females, left the countryside to find employment in the industrial towns and cities where better paid factory or domestic work was available. A lot of work was available in the Cambridge Colleges and on their estates around Cambridge. For those who were unable to leave, some manifested their dissatisfaction with the state of affairs by acts of vandalism. This period, known as "The Swing" after the number of hangings of offenders, saw incidences of farm machinery being destroyed, windows broken and haystacks, barns and even farmers' houses being set alight. (Fowle, K. (19--), 'Coton through the Ages') However, the discovery of the fossil seam reduced this unrest.

As shall be seen, this dissatisfaction diminished during the coprolite years with higher wages and a variety of new jobs available. What were these coprolites? "Coprolites," as they were called when they were first discovered, were thought to be fossilised droppings. There are numerous variations of their spelling, due in part to the poor literacy of the census enumerator but also to variations in local dialect. They include coprolite, copperlight, copper light, copperlite, coupperlite, copralite, coprollate, corporolite, coprelite, coperlite, coporlite, coparlite, coprolithe and coperalite. No wonder there was confusion over their origin. (Analysis of the 1861 – 1891 census data) The word came from the Greek "kopros" meaning dung and "lithos" meaning stone. Dung stone - fossilised droppings!

Rev. William Buckland, the Dean of Westminster, was the first to coin when he was Oxford University's first professor of Geology and Mineralogy. In 1829 he went on a geological excursion to the Dorset coast at Lyme Regis. Examining the clay and sands exposed by a recent landslip he found the complete fossil remains of an ichthyosaurus. Unusually, it also included its fossilised stomach contents.

Accompanying him on the excursion was the German analytical chemist, Baron Von Justus Liebig. He too was fascinated with the finds but the Dean was obsessed. He had a table top inlaid with polished coprolites as well as earrings made from polished slices! It is unknown if he wore them! His dinner parties were very entertaining. A bear used to wander around the dining room behind his guests and a monkey sat on furniture near the window. The menu often included samples from across the food chain, starting from plants and working through the animal kingdom! The worst tasting were reportedly moles and bluebottles! Dinnertime conversations included a challenge to the established religious circles. Buckland had found tiny bones of baby ichthyosaurus in the coprolites. This meant that ichthyosaurus ate ichthyosaurus. They were cannibals! This contradicted the fundamental religious belief that life before Adam was one of peace and harmony. Presumably it was believed that Adam and Eve frolicked with dinosaurs in Eden. Maybe the issue was discussed over dinner with Mr and Mrs Mantell who were the first to find Iguanodon remains in Sussex in 1822 and Sir Richard Owen who first came up with the word dinosaur to mean "terrible lizard". Owen was just as eccentric. On New Year's Eve 1853 he invited twenty scientists to a dinner party inside a life-size model of an iguanodon in a London park!

A similar discovery but one with far reaching implications was made in 1842. After Rev. John Henslow, the professor of Botany at St. John's College, Cambridge had been given a living by St. John's in the Suffolk parish of Hitcham, he went on a trip to the Victorian watering hole of Felixstowe. There had

Rev. William Buckland, (1784 – 1856), Dean of Westminster, curator of Ashmolean Museum, Oxford, President of Geological Society. He coined the word coprolite after finding a complete fossil of an ichthyosaurus at Lyme Regis. (www.pengellytrust.org/museum/paleontology.htm)

Rev. John Henslow (1786 – 1861), Professor of Mineralogy, St John's Cambridge., vicar of Hitcham, Suffolk. He found what he thought were coprolites in a cliff collapse at Felixstow and recommended Ipswich manure manufacturers use them. (www.freightmatters.co.uk/suffolkarch/news21.htm

recently been a landslip in which he found some interesting fossils in the newly exposed material at the bottom of the cliffs. There were loads of them. From their smooth, brown, elongated shape he took them to be fossilised dung, similar to those of the ichthyosaurus, discovered by Buckland. (O'Connor, B. (1998), 'Felixstowe's Fossil Industry', Bernard O'Connor, Everton) Aware that a range of animal products was being used as manure he wondered what possible use these fossils could have.

Liebig had done some tests on Buckland's coprolites by dissolving them in vitriol, the then term for sulphuric acid. His analysis of the resultant mass showed them to have a high phosphate content, a mineral much needed in plant growth. John Bennet Lawes, a Hertfordshire landowner, was experimenting with different manures on his estate in Rothamsted. Like Liebig, he too successfully dissolved animal bones, the mineral phosphorite and Felixstowe coprolites in vitriol. The resulting mixture, once dried and bagged, he called "super phosphate of lime". His tests showed that it was soluble in water and that the plant roots could rapidly absorb it. He experimented with it on plants in pots and test beds showed it to be an extremely valuable manure, especially for root crops. His "super" was the world's first artificial chemical manure and its application so dramatically increased turnip yields that it became much in demand by the nation's farmers. They were eager to improve supplies of winter fodder. This was because once the harvest was in and farmers knew how much winter feed was available, large numbers of surplus cattle, sheep or pigs had to be slaughtered. Meat commanded higher prices over winter until the new stock was brought onto the market in spring. Any way of providing increased fodder therefore would be very popular with farmers.

Much to Lawes' pleasure the results of his tests with his new manure showed that it was effective on a whole range of other crops. He patented his "discovery" in 1842, which annoyed Liebig who claimed to have been the first to have done it. It also upset Lawes' mother who was appalled that a gentleman should engage in trade - let alone in manure. Ignoring both he set up his own company. It was called "Lawes Artificial Manure Company." His fiancée could not have been pleased. The planned European Tour for their honeymoon was cancelled in favour of a trip down the Thames during which he spotted an ideal site for his factory. He bought a plot at Deptford and had a large chemical manure works built that was capable of producing up to 200 tons of superphosphate a week. He sold his "super" at up to £7.00 and took legal action against Liebig and others to ensure that anyone who wanted to use his patent had to pay him five shillings (£0.25) for every ton they produced. (Dyke, G.V. (1993), 'John Lawes of Rothamsted' Hoos Press, Harpenden, p.15)

Maybe Henslow was in correspondence with Lawes as he realised that the Felixstowe fossil bed could be a valuable source of manure. As a wide range of animal manure was being put onto the fields he thought that fossilised droppings could be used for the same purpose. In 1845 he read a paper in Cambridge to the British Association for the Advancement of Science. (Henslow, Rev. John, (1845), Report to British Association, Cambridge) It dealt with their potential value to the nation's farmers. Suffolk manure manufacturers like William Colchester, Edward Packard and Joseph Fison took interest. They made arrangements with Felixstowe landowners to have the fossils dug up, washed and transported to their works in Ipswich. A few shillings a ton royalty was offered for the fossils. As a cheap alternative to the other manures on the market, there was keen interest in coprolites.

The 18th and 19th century exodus from the countryside to the urban areas resulted in an enormous demand for accommodation and food. The ending of the Napoleonic Wars with the defeat of the French at Waterloo in 1815 brought a period of peace and prosperity to Britain. Its population doubled over the first half of the century. Towns and cities expanded rapidly on the coalfields and alongside the major rivers and canal system. People were attracted by the employment opportunities in industry, retail and commerce following the inventions of the Industrial Revolution. There were also many forced off the land by developments in the Agricultural revolution. The urban population needed feeding. The typical two-up two-down terraced houses didn't have the gardens to grow fruit or vegetables or space to keep a pig or chickens. People needed to buy food from the High Street, the market or the corner shops. Victorian entrepreneurs were quick to recognise the growing demand. Small family businesses dominated the business. As their profits grew they opened more shops, invested in better transport and had more money to buy from the farmers. If farmers could increase production there was more money to be made. Experiments began in an attempt to increase food production.

One can probably remember from one's schooldays Jethro Tull's seed drill, Lord 'Turnip' Townsend's four-course crop rotation method and the Earl of Norfolk and other agriculturalists' crossbreeding produced enormous pigs, cattle and sheep. But other experiments were going on with plants. The application of science and capital was being expended on agriculture as it had been on manufacturing. Once the chemists acknowledged that phosphate was a major nutrient in plant growth, the search was on to discover new supplies. In 1828 a rock phosphate, called phosphorite, started being exploited in Ontario, Canada. Chemists had found its value as a fertiliser and samples were tested in Great Britain. The German explorer, Humboldt, returned to Europe with details of the South American coastline and his report led to the European's "discovering" the use of "huano" or guano. This was an accumulation of tens of feet of phosphate-rich bird droppings that had impregnated discarded fish carcasses and bird skeletons on the Chincha Islands off the coast of Peru. The locals would not excavate it because of the smell so indentured Chinese labour was brought in. Shipping companies started to import it into Liverpool docks from 1838 where it was sold it at up to £12 per ton. This was much more expensive than bones but a successful advertising campaign in the agricultural press led to its widespread usage.

Other experiments included adding a whole range of materials to the soil. Blood, bones, soot, fish, seaweed, chalk, clay and even rags from discarded wool and cotton clothes were trialled. Maybe one can remember the rag and bone man? It was the waste product of the knife manufacturers in Sheffield, however, that sparked the interest in bones. It was found that the shavings from their knife handles proved a very effective fertiliser when added to the soil. (Voelcker, A. (1862), 'The International Exhibition at Paris,' p.149) The corn mills used by the agricultural suppliers were not able to meet the demand for bone meal and this led to the setting up of bone manure works. Their most popular products were half-inch bones. These were burnt or crushed and added to the soil as bone meal.

However, the bones from the knacker's yards were insufficient to meet the demand of the nation's manure manufacturers, a factor that led to the import of dried bones. There were reports of cargoes of mummified cats from Egyptian pyramids and sun-bleached bones from the North African desert and the Argentinean Pampas finding their way into the crushing mills. This was enough to prompt the comment by Baron Von Justus Liebig, that,

> *"Great Britain is like a ghoul, searching the continents for bones to feed its agriculture ... robbing all other countries of the condition of her fertility. Already in her eagerness for bones she has turned up the battlefields of Leipzig, Waterloo, and of the Crimea; already from the catacombs of Sicily she has carried away the skeletons of many successive generations."*

(Quoted in Keatley, W.S. (1976), '100 years of Fertiliser Manufacture,' Fertiliser Manufacturers Association; also in Pierre, W.H. and Norman, A.G. (Eds.) (1953), 'Soil Fertiliser Phosphorous in Crop Nutrition,' New York Academic Press, p. ix)

By 1839 the bone business was worth £150,000 per annum and about 30,000 tons were being imported annually. The Gardeners' and Agricultural Gazette gave detailed accounts of the efficacy of these new manures. (Graham, J. (1839), 'A Treatise on the Use and Value of Manure', London p.6) However, tests showed that crushed bones were insoluble. It also took a long time before their mineral potential could be absorbed. Bones were also expensive and the machinery for grinding them had not been perfected. (Ibid.)

Maybe it was the reports of Rev. Henslow's speech that prompted a local farmer to show him some fossils that he had dug up on his property. Charles Kingsley, one of Henslow's students, must have been present as he recorded Henslow's response.

> "He saw, being somewhat of, a geologist and chemist, that they were not, as fossils usually are, carbonate of lime, but phosphate of lime - bone earth. He said at once, as by inspiration, "You have found a treasure - not a gold-mine, indeed, but a food-mine. This bone earth, which we are at our wit's end to get for our grain and pulses; which we are importing, as expensive bones, all the way from Buenos Ayres. Only find enough of them, and you will increase immensely the food supply of England and perhaps make her independent of foreign phosphates in case of war."

(Anonymous note in Ipswich Museum's Coprolite file)

A treasure? A food-mine? Such a response must have astounded the farmer. It is undocumented where the farmer was from but it is thought that he was from Burwell, a fenland parish north of Cambridge. Fossils had been found beneath the fenland peat from as early as 1816. (Hailstone, Rev. J. (1816), 'Outlines of the Geology of Cambridgeshire', Phil. Trans. Royal. Soc., pp.243-250) Their discovery was related to an important fenland occupation, locally called "claying". This involved the digging of small pits through the "moor" or "bear's muck", as the bog-earth was called, to reach the clay. This lay between two and ten feet (0.74m. - 3.7m.) below the surface. Wearing waterproofed boots the diggers would use a sharp, cutting-edged shovel to dig through the peat, a light wooden scoop to get rid of drainage water and an axe or "bill" to excavate the clay beneath. The top metre of clay was thrown to the sides of the pit and then mixed into the peat.

The material turned up by this "claying" occasionally included fossils of what were thought to be bears and oxen. When Burwell Fen started to be drained in the early-1800s the excavation of drainage ditches or "lodes" exposed an extensive bed of fossils. A local farmer, John Ball, noticed that the turnips he grew on the clayey, fossil deposit that had been mixed into his peat soil produced dramatically better yields than the crops on fields he had not clayed. The Burwell doctor, Mr. Lucas, explained that the "extraordinary liveliness" was related to the high phosphate content of the fossils. ('The Farming of Cambridgeshire,' Royal Agric.Soc.1847, p.71; Lucas, C. (1930), 'The Fenman's World - Memories of a Fenland Physician,' (Norwich), p.25)

Dr. Lucas may well have heard about Rev. Henslow's Cambridge speech or read about it in the local press. Aware of the potential demand by manure manufacturers and maybe even knowing the farmer who had shown Henslow the fossils, he suspected that the Burwell deposit could also be a matter of "commercial proposition". Their shallow depth beneath the fenland peat just above the gault clay would allow them to be raised without very high labour costs. The proximity of Burwell Lode allowed easy access by barge or lighter to Popes Corner - the confluence of the Ouse and the Cam - and then via Ely, Littleport and Downham Market onto King's Lynn and then transhipped to Ipswich or London.

With an eye for speculation and without having first seen it, he bought some eleven acres of Burwell Fen. The locals thought he had taken leave of his senses. A month later, so the story goes, he went by boat up Burwell Lode with "an interested party" to locate the deposit. After rowing for some time, they reached a point about a mile west of the village where the potential buyer was handed a "sprit" and told to push it into the land below the boat. (Gathercole, A. F. (1959), 'Fenland Village,' Fisons Journal, No.64 Sept. pp.24-9; Suffolk County Record Office (SCRO) HC 438.8728/269)

The depth of the seam was not noted but the locals were astounded when he sold the plot and the coprolites beneath it for £1,000. Realising almost £100 per acre was a phenomenal profit, given that agricultural rents at this time ranged from about ten to forty shillings (£0.50 - £2.00) an acre. The "interested party" was William Colchester, one of the Suffolk manure manufacturers who also had investments in brick manufacturing and ships. In 1846 he expanded his manure business by building a new manure works in Ipswich. According to a later geological paper he had raised 500 tons by 1847. (Lucas, C. (1930), op.cit; Reid, C. (1890), 'Nodule Bed,' Memoirs of the Geological Survey (MGS), p.16)

Others speculated in the new industry. Edward Packard, a chemist from Saxmundham in Suffolk successfully processed the Felixstowe "coprolites" and in 1847 he opened his own manure factory on the banks of the River Orwell in Ipswich. Joseph Fison, part of a milling and baking family, had moved into Ipswich in 1840. He established a factory at Stoke Bridge and converted it to process coprolites and other phosphatic material in 1850. (Fisons Journal, No.77,December 1963; Norsk Hydro file, Museum of East Anglian Life, Stowmarket)

Lawes, Colchester, Packard and Fison advertised their superphosphate in the pages of the "Gardeners Chronicle and Agricultural Gazette" thus realising Henslow's idea. Articles on its successful application and of using coprolites in its manufacture appeared in the agricultural press. These increased landowners and agriculturalists' awareness of the financial advantages of locating the fossil deposit on their properties.

By the 1850s Buckland realised that his discovery had led to the birth of a new industry exploiting fossil beds in Suffolk and Cambridgeshire. He questioned the possibility that these

"...excretions of extinct animals contained the mineral ingredients of so much value in animal manure. The question was in fact not yet solved by the chemist, and we took specimens, in order to confirm by chemical analysis the views of the geologist. After Liebig had completed their analysis, he saw that they might be made applicable to practical purposes.

What a curious and interesting subject for contemplation! In the remains of an extinct animal world England is to find the means of increasing her wealth in agricultural produce, as she has already found the great support of her manufacturing industry in fossil fuel - the preserved matter of primeval forests - the remains of a vegetable world! May this expectation be realised! and may her excellent population be thus redeemed from poverty and misery!

I well recollect the storm of ridicule raised by these expressions of the German philosopher, and yet truth has triumphed over scepticism, and thousands of tons of similar animal remains are now used in promoting the fertility of our fields. The geological observer, in his search after evidences of ancient life, aided by the chemist, excavated extinct remains which produced new life to future generations."

(Anonymous author, 'The Study of Abstract Science Essential to the Progress of Industry,' MGS, Mineral Statistics, vol. I, 1850?, pp.40-1)

Many people thought that the fossils were the droppings of bear, lizard or fish or even dinosaur droppings. A retired major from Reach thought that they resembled sun-dried wildebeest droppings. They were similar to those he had seen on the banks of the Zambezi once the vast herds had passed. Students and professors at Cambridge University's newly established Geology department became very interested in the range of fossils being thrown up. There was extensive debate in geological circles and many argued that the deposit ought not to be termed coprolite. They should more correctly be termed pseudo-coprolites or phosphatic nodules. However, the trade name "coprolites" stuck. Recently however, an excellent example of some poor creature's rectal content has been found in Barrington that gives credence to the locals' views. One can make out the pressure creases and a sharp point as if it was its last squeeze. Photographs of this and typical Cambridgeshire coprolites can be seen on page ..

The bulk of the deposit was of misshapen, black/grey lumps but amongst them were found the teeth, bones, scales and claws of prehistoric creatures such as Cretaceous dinosaurs. They included craterosaurus, dakosaurus, dinotosaurus, megalosaurus, iguanodon and the pterodactyl. Prehistoric marine reptiles of ichthyosaurus, plesiosaurus and pliosaurus were found as well as the remains of whale, shark, turtle and a huge variety of shells, sponges and other marine organisms. The most common was the ammonite. Other animals that were discovered in the diggings included crocodile, hippopotamus, elephant, rhinoceros, lion, hyena, tapir, bear, horse and oxen. (O'Connor, B. (1998), 'The Dinosaurs on Sandy Heath', Bernard O'Connor, Everton) There were also lumps of what some argue are inorganic calcium phosphate. But why is it that such a variety of creatures that you would normally expect to see in hot tropical countries in Africa were found in Cambridgeshire?

When the European plate broke away from Pangaea about 500 million years ago it was south of the Equator. It was during this period that the gault clay was deposited. This area was about 28° S, where Namibia is today! To reach its present latitude about 55° N it experienced a range of differing environments on its slow movement north from the tropical and equatorial forests, swamps, savannah grassland and desert to the temperate latitudes. But what had produced such an enormous prehistoric graveyard? A number of the Victorian geologists considered that the Jurassic and Cretaceous fossil deposits had been washed out of the clays which were exposed when the south of England was uplifted from the sea to produce the Weald. A recent theory is that about 94 million years ago sea levels rose dramatically, flooding the London-Brabant Basin, of which present day Cambridgeshire formed its northern coast. This wiped out much of the animal population. Carbon dioxide given off by the flood basalts released by the tectonic activity also played their part. Many of the land creatures would have been poisoned and also the marine life that had to come up to the surface for air. Some suggested that as the bodies accumulated as debris in coastal embayments their bones, teeth, scales and claws gradually absorbed the phosphoric acid from overlying deposits of decaying organisms. Another theory was that the calcium absorbed dissolved phosphate from the seawater. It was said that the rivers had dissolved the apatite, a phosphatic mineral found in the volcanic rocks of Scandinavia and Scotland, which impregnated the deposit and explains their higher phosphate content than today's animal and human bones.

Analysis of amber samples shows that at the time when dinosaurs were at their greatest size, about 230 million years ago, the oxygen content of the air was 35%. Over the Cretaceous period it gradually declined as a result of the increased carbon dioxide released into the atmosphere by extensive volcanic activity. Levels fell to 11% 65 million years ago and today they are 21%. Dinosaurs had to adapt to these changing conditions. It was like having asthma, not getting enough oxygen into the blood. They had to build enough energy to catch prey - the "dash and dine" characteristic of today's crocodiles. Many were exhausted, maybe too tired for sex even. Like crocodiles they buried their eggs. It is thought that increased temperatures meant that they had single-sex populations that further reduced numbers. The leathery skin of their eggs absorbed the poisonous gases and embryos failed to develop. In order to survive these changing conditions dinosaurs had to evolve with a much-reduced size. A cataclysmic catastrophe like a rise in sea level of hundreds of feet as well as poisoned air could explain the huge numbers of creatures found in the East Anglian fossil beds. Given the volume of the creatures they must have piled up on each other into a layer many tens of feet thick in hollows on the seabed. The upper bodies would have been eaten by any of the surviving marine life like ammonites and worms but the lower bodies, without oxygen for decomposition, gradually fossilised as the upper layers were covered in the hundreds of feet of Cambridgeshire Greensand. This was probably washed into the ocean from the arid parts of continent still above sea level.

Compressed by this strata and the subsequent chalk marl of Eastern and Southern Cambridgeshire they gradually fossilised. This could explain why there are real coprolites in the deposit. The contents of stomachs, intestines and rectums would have been found along with bones, teeth, claws, scales and shells. Throughout the deposit were large numbers of ammonites, squid-like creatures that scavenged on the sea floor but there were oyster shells on the upper surface. Over the millions of years, fluctuations in sea level exposed the soft Greensand and differential erosion uncovered the fossils at its base. The remains would have been washed around, so that one does not find whole skeletons in the deposit. Many of the surface features of the remains were removed by abrasion but lines showing worm tracks are often visible along the nodules, the biggest of which rarely extend over six inches (15cms).

Further inundation resulted in a second bed accumulating which was covered once more with Greensand deposits and then hundreds of feet of chalk. This latter deposit was made up from minute marine organisms whose bodies contained calcium carbonate. When sea levels eventually fell, these more recent deposits were exposed to the elements. The upper layers would have been eroded and the chalk and sand gradually lowered to expose the fossil beds. The sixteen ice ages contributed most to the erosion removing hundreds of feet of rock to leave the low chalk and sandy ridges of East Anglia.

Whilst the bed was one of great fascination to the country's geologists, its commercial value was not in how much they could be sold to those Victorians fascinated by fossils. Another of Rev. Henslow's students at Cambridge was Charles Darwin. His evolutionary theories caused a storm when they were published in 1858 and further stimulated the enormous interest in geology, palaeontology, anthropology and archaeology. Many Victorian drawing rooms had specimens from the Greensand displayed in glass-sided cabinets. They were also eagerly bought up by geology students and their professors as well as by museum curators across the country. Perhaps the best specimens can be found in the Sedgwick Earth Sciences Museum in Cambridge.

Their main value, however, was as a raw material for manure manufacturers. And not just in this country but also overseas. In the late-1840s they were paying landowners as little as a few shillings a ton for them. As more and more businesses joined in the rush for manures, demand for coprolite rose. Royalties they paid landowners rose to between seven and fifteen shillings (£0.35 - £0.75) a ton in the early 1850s. They depended on a range of factors. The depth, extent, continuity of the seam, the angle of dip, its cleanliness, the nearness to a water source, road, wharf or station, the volume coming onto the market, knowledge or ignorance of current prices and, inevitably, nepotism - how well the contractor knew the landowner.

A new extractive industry began - an alternative and much more profitable line of work than digging clunch, clay or turf. When the fossil seam was noticed in the Chesterton brick fields in 1848 the owners sold some of what they considered "troublesome annoyances" to Mr. Deck, a chemist of Fitzroy Street, Cambridge for £2 per ton. He probably was not told the royalties the Suffolk manure manufacturers were paying but would have known that similar "phosphatic nodules" were being raised in the Felixstowe and Burwell areas. His tests done on them showed that the Cambridgeshire "coprolites" had between 50% - 60% calcium phosphate, up to 10% higher than the Suffolk variety. It stimulated their extraction as *"a matter of commercial proposition."* (Cambridge Independent Press, 18th January, p.3)

When it was found that the seam extended to the south under Coldham's Common in Barnwell, the industry took off on a large scale. Some Suffolk manure manufacturers and entrepreneurial coprolite contractors, keen to capitalise on the demand, moved into the area to win agreements with brickyard and other landowners to raise the fossils. Gangs of experienced diggers came over to run the Cambridgeshire pits from Suffolk and other counties. (O'Connor, B. (1998), 'The Dinosaurs on Coldham's Common', Bernard O'Connor, Everton) This in-migration was not evidenced in the 1851 census, however. There was no reference to fossil or coprolite diggers, coprolite contractors or merchants in any of the parishes where it was then being worked. It is thought that the work was just considered as labouring or, if they were employed by a farmer, as agricultural labour.

It was hardly a coincidence that the geological mapping of the country started around this time. Whilst the exploration was mainly for scientific reasons, knowledge of the extent and distribution of the Greensand was of commercial importance to those who had money to invest in what was to become known as the coprolite diggings.

Averaging about 30 inches thick (about 39 cm.) in places the seam was up to six feet (2.1 metres). In some areas it was non-existent, locally called "dead land", due to a slight rise in the seabed whilst the fossils had tended to accumulate in the hollows. Yields therefore varied. In Cambridge itself it was about 300 tons per acre (0.404ha.). In one pit in Wicken it was 2,000 tons but the average was 250 tons per acre. (Kingston, A. (1889) 'Old and New Industries on the Cam.' Warren Press, Royston p.16) When annual agricultural rents were rarely over fifty shillings (£2.50) an acre and these coprolites could be sold at over £2.00 per ton, potentially several hundred pounds could be realised from an acre! Wages of agricultural labourers at that time wouldn't have been over £25 in a year and £200 could have bought a small estate. No wonder there was a lot of interest in them. So began what was termed by the historian, Richard Grove, as "The Cambridgeshire Coprolite Mining Rush." (Oleander Press, Cambridge, 1976)

The depth and extent of the bed had to be determined. This was done initially by digging a coffin-like pit. A cheaper method was by using a two-man corkscrew borer. Walter Tye, in his account of the Suffolk industry included an interview with one of the diggers who said that

> "To test the depth of the coprolite he made use of a tool like a giant corkscrew, called a 'dipper,' which shuddered in his hands when striking the mineral. Local cottagers always knew what the foreman was after when he came into their gardens carrying his 'dipper.' Naturally, they strongly objected to their gardens being turned topsy-turvy, however much coprolite he might find there, and they were always delighted to see him go. Old residents today say that a sixpenny tip usually had the desired effect."
>
> Tye, Walter (1930),'Birth of the Fertilizer Industry', Fisons Journal, p.8.)

In places the deposit was found outcropping on the surface but in most cases it had to be dug from between ten and twenty feet (3.7 – 7.4m.) of chalk marl. Where it was found on a small property it was simple matter for the landowner to take on a gang of labourers and have the fossils dug up, washed and sorted and then carted off and sold to a manure manufacturer. In this case it was commonly the farmer's own agricultural labourers. They used to dig the fossils during the low season, once the harvest was in. The work continued over the winter months and then the pits would be left to allow the farm work to start in spring.

If the land was copyhold then the tenant might get permission to raise it using their labourers but occasionally, where a large-scale operation was envisaged, they were evicted and a coprolite manager allowed to move in to the farmhouse. On larger properties an advertisement might be placed in the local press and tenders invited for a contractor to do the work. This occasionally led to existing tenants being given notice to quit to allow the coprolite manager a house to live in whilst the works were in operation but, more often than not, they were compensated for the loss of revenue from those fields which were being dug. Farmers and others set themselves up as coprolite contractors and took on a gang of men and boys. Pick axes, crowbars, shovels, planks, dog irons (supports for the planks), wheelbarrows, trucks and tramway had to be bought and a horse or steam-operated washmill had to be erected to clean the soil and clay from the fossils. A tool shed was erected and another for sorting, having lunch or sheltering from the rain. All this cost money and local bank managers were keen to make loans to enterprising individuals in an industry that had such high returns.

Women and girls were employed in large numbers where the deposit was found in sandier areas. Here the fossils needed sorting to remove any unwanted stones that would reduce the quality and therefore the price paid by the manure manufacturers. There is no evidence of any female employment in the Hauxton area. The main female employment was in Wicken in the fens and Potton, near Sandy in Bedfordshire.

Contractors agreed to do the work over a set number of years with them paying the landowner a royalty of so much per ton. The tenant farmer was often compensated for the loss of revenue from those fields out of cultivation by up to £10 an acre. Once work got started the topsoil and subsoil was barrowed to one side of the field to be replaced later. In many cases it was used as the base of the washmill. As the coprolite seam was exposed the diggers shovelled it into wheelbarrows or emptied it into trucks. These were then pushed by hand or pulled by horses along a tramway that ran out of the pit, along the edge of the field or trackway to the washmill. Here their contents were unloaded to create large piles before they were washed and sorted. The soil above the seam on the new face was removed after undercutting, a process which caused considerable danger. Crowbars, pick-axes and shovels were used to make it collapse and, for convenience, it was just thrown into the trench already worked. As shall be seen there were numerous cases of accidents in the pits caused by collapses. This "backfilling" meant that the labourers gradually progressed across the field and onto adjoining property where a new lease was sought. Where another contractor had workings in neighbouring fields pits were opened at opposite ends of the field and two gangs of diggers gradually dug their way towards each other.

The job of washing the fossils got progressively easier over the years. Initially the technique in Suffolk was to dig a trench into the side of the estuary or the river. The actual washing and screening process down at the dock was described in Walter Tye's fascinating insights into the diggings.

"That was an old man's job when he became too old for the pit. A long tank some thirty feet in length, was specially provided for the job. The coprolites, along with a certain amount of dirt and bones, were shovelled into sieves which, when full, were placed on a ledge in the tank, just under the surface of the water; to each sieve was fastened a long pole, which the washer pulled backwards and forwards until the stones were clean. When there was a shortage of water, in or near the pit, the washing was done at the quayside before loading."

(Tye, W. op.cit)

In Cambridgeshire, without access to a tidal estuary, innovative engineers used their skills to develop sophisticated washmills powered by horse or steam engine. A mound was constructed using the top and subsoil. On top of this mound a circular brick base was laid onto which a circular iron tray was placed. Large sections of the iron plates that formed the base of one such washmill have been found on Rectory Farm, Whaddon. Barrow-loads of fossils were wheeled up the mound and emptied into the tray. A pump was often installed to bring the huge quantities of water needed from a nearby water source. Wells sometimes had to be dug and lined with bricks. At one time there were eleven such mills in operation in the Bassingbourn area which were claimed to have been responsible for lowing the water table of the area. (Whitaker, W. (1921), 'Water Supply of Cambs.' MGS, London, p 84; A photograph of one of the harrows used can be seen in the Cambridgeshire Collection W27.1. KO. 19554)

The working of these mills was described by the son of the Burwell doctor, Mr Lucas, whose coprolite land was the first to exploited in Cambridgeshire-. Once the coprolite had been brought to the surface: -

"*The first thing to do was to throw up a hill in the middle of the ground, and this was done by first erecting a post about ten or twelve feet long, and throwing the soil around it to a height of eleven or twelve feet and of thirty feet in diameter. Three feet from the centre a ring would be formed six to eight feet wide and four feet deep. This would be paved with bricks and the sides would be sheets of iron. On one side of the hill a platform was made from a wooden tank, to which was connected a pump eighteen feet long; a pipe from the tank would go with the ring and opposite the tank was a trapped outlet, and on the outer side of the hill a square of about two chains would be earthed up a little to form a sort of pan. From the central post a wooden arm would be attached about twelve to fourteen feet long; to this would be attached a wimpole tree, to which a horse would be yoked. Connected to the centre of the post would be a light rail which was fixed to the horse bridle to keep the horse always in is track; from the arm would be suspended two iron harrows which ran well in on the bottom of the ring. When the soil containing the fossils was wheeled up to the ring a sufficient quantity of water would be let in. As the horse went round a creamy fluid would be produced and the fossils would drop on the floor. Then the trapped outlet would be opened and the creamlike fluid, called "slurry" would flow into pans. This operation having been repeated a number of times the fossils on the floor would be washed clear of earth and weighed up*".

(Lucas, C. op.cit. p.31)

The cost of constructing these mills in the late-1840s when they were first developed was £100 but by 1875 the "*coprolite contractors had become so expeditious that a hill could be put up for £5!* (Ibid.) A description of such mills was recorded in a tourist's account of a trip in the fens.

> *"As we return from Burwell our eyes rest on several raised circular enclosures, round which a number of often grey horses are almost ceaselessly walking. These are the mills erected for washing the fossils. These fossils or coprolites are valuable on account of the calcic phosphate contained in them."*

(Eade, David, (18--), 'Rambles in Cambridgeshire', Soham, p.48)

As the technology improved, those contractors who could afford them introduced steam-powered washmills. After several washings the dirty water, locally termed "slub" or "slurry" was run back into "slurry pans" to dry out before the topsoil was replaced. The theory was that once dried the cracks in it would allow better drainage. As the work progressed across the field the mill was transferred to a more accessible site. The topsoil was barrowed back into the trench or slurry pit and levelled ready for cultivation. Whilst the theory was that this process would improve the soil, in practise the operation was not always done thoroughly. It was cheaper for a contractor to cover it up quickly and move on. A farmer, however, would take care, as he would benefit from improved cropping. In several areas white chalk markings can still be seen on the fields which indicate where slurry was not properly covered or the topsoil replaced. Astute land agents ensured that agreements included very precise instructions for this process and subsequent drainage, levelling and seeding.

Horses would have been a common sight hauling tumbrils loaded with washed coprolites along the country lanes to Harston Station on the Hitchin to Cambridge branch of the Eastern Counties Railway. Some went to Meldreth or Royston stations or north to Lord's Bridge Station near Barton. Loaded into low, drop-sided trucks with COPROLITES painted in red on the side, they were taken to manure factories in Cambridge, Ipswich, London and elsewhere. Rev. Jenyns, the vicar of Bottisham and Charles Darwin's tutor at Cambridge, pointed out that

> *"After drying and weighing, they are taken to the railway Station and sent up to London. Whole strings of trucks full of*

them may often be seen at Cambridge, the trucks being kept for this traffic and labelled accordingly, the number of them indicating the largeness of the business for which they are set apart."

(Jenyns, Rev. L. (1866), 'On the Phosphatic Nodules obtained in the Eastern Counties, and used in Agriculture.' Proceedings Bath Natural History Field Club p.17)

Some were carted direct to local bone mills like Walton's on East Road in Cambridge or the Cambridge Manure Company's works on Histon Road. This company was set up in the early-1850s by the Cambridge auctioneer, John Rolfe Mann, a Fulbourn merchant, A. P. Chaplin, and other "agriculturalists" and entrepreneurs who recognised the profits to be made in this lucrative business. Clement Francis, a Cambridge solicitor, was to act as their "undisclosed agent." (Cambridge Collection, Cooper's Misc. Papers, 32. 1856; Cambridgeshire County Record Office (CCRO) Francis & Co. Bill Books, 1855 pp.455,539; CCRO R60/3 Cambridge Manure Co. Minute Books.) Many local bone and corn mills had to be converted as the gritstone was not hard enough to grind the coprolites. A hard buhrstone had to be installed in its place. Whether the mills at Hauxton were used for this purpose has not been documented. There were other manure works in Hallack and Bond's siding by Cambridge railway station and behind Headly's iron works on Mill Road. Some would have been carted into Cambridge. There was a wharf at Silver Street Bridge where, loaded onto a barge or fenland lighter, they could be taken up the Cam and Ouse to King's Lynn for transhipment round the coast.

When records show that coprolites were being sold to the manufacturers in the late-1850s as high as thirty-nine shillings and sixpence (£1.97) per ton and yields around Cambridge averaged 300 tons an acre, one can understand why many people were keen to set themselves up as coprolite contractors and coprolite merchants. With "super" being sold at up to £7 a ton, half the price of guano, it became much in demand across the country. It was not long therefore before sales were being promoted across Europe, in America and throughout the Empire. There were reports of sales as far afield as Russia and Queensland. (O'Connor, B. (1998) 'The Dinosaurs on Coldham's Common', Bernard O'Connor, Everton) During the 1850s there were four manure factories in Cambridge. With them paying an average forty-three shillings and sixpence (£2.18) a ton in 1856 for Cambridge coprolites there were profits to be made by coprolite contractors and merchants.

Being paid by the ton necessitated having a weighbridge set up by the field gate at the entrance to the works and for accurate measurements to be recorded. There were claims of carts being sent underweight. To avoid errors and dependence on the contractors' weighings the land agents suggested an alternative scheme whereby royalties should be paid according to how many acres were dug over the year. This entailed having the pits surveyed around Lady Day (May 1st) and Michaelmas (September 29th). The surveyor's measurements could then be used to determine how much the contractor owed. This provided local companies like Bidwell, Francis, Smith, Carter Jonas and Mann and Raven a valuable additional source of income for the next forty years. Royalties ranged from as high as £400 to as low as £30 an acre but the average was about £100. This was about forty to fifty times the revenue the landowners could get from agricultural rents. After plant, machinery, royalties and labour costs were deducted the contractors could make a big profit.

The rush to locate these profitable beds stimulated the geological mapping of the county. In fact, the deposit had been mapped in most of the Eastern Counties by the 1870s. Although the two seams were not continuous, the Greensand fossils were worked from parts of Suffolk, Norfolk, Cambridgeshire, Hertfordshire, Bedfordshire, Buckinghamshire, Oxfordshire, Hampshire, Yorkshire and Kent. Its enormous extent allowed many new manure companies to capitalise on this new raw material and take a share of the increasing market for artificial fertilisers. Accordingly, many new chemical manure works were opened on the coprolite belt in Cambridge, Burwell, Duxford, Shepreth, Royston, Bassingbourn and Odsey near Ashwell.

Throughout the 1850s the seam was worked in Cambridge itself. Many of the open fields around the town were dug, not just for the coprolites but also for gravel and clay. There was a housing boom in the towns which stimulated the construction industry. With the development of mass-production in the brick and tile making industry, landowners were able to bring a lot more clay land under cultivation. This was done by laying down drainage tiles. The trenching work for this, or deep ploughing, often revealed the coprolite seam a few feet below the surface. By 1856 it had been discovered along the foot of Coton Ridge, just west of Cambridge. Work started at the same time in fields east of Barton, in Little Eversden and Orwell where it was found around the edges of several low hills of chalk marl that overlay the gault clay. (Kelly's Post Office Directory, Orwell, 1864; Kelly's Post Office Directory, Little Eversden, 1869) In his historical account of Wimpole, the vicar, Rev. A.C. Yorke, nephew of Charles Phillip Yorke, the 5th Earl of Hardwicke, stated that the coprolite digging, *"somewhere about 1856 forced its way onto the Wimpole estates."* (Cambridge University Library, (CUL.) Palmer Papers B51, Yorke, A.C. (1979), 'Wimpole as I knew it,' p.12; Pennings and Jukes-Brown, (1881), 'Geology of the Neighbourhood of Cambridge' HMSO. p.38)

One of Cambridge's iron founders, James Ind Headly, who built the famous Eagle steam engine, was very much involved in the coprolite business. He had his own coprolite works erected behind his Eagle Foundry on Mill Road in Cambridge and had his works, *"well fitted up to make the pumps, washmills, cast iron screens and steam engines to provide power."* (Enid Porter's notebooks Cambridge Folk Museum 15/64-65) He was aware of the investment opportunities in this area and luck had it that one of his relatives lived in Coton whose land was dug for coprolites. Over the next few decades he was to become of the leading coprolite contractors in this area.

In this area the seam was found along the 50-foot (16m.) contour line which ran around the slopes of "Money Hill" in Haslingfield. Maybe drainage work had uncovered it? The earliest evidence was in February 1857. Earl De La Warr, an absentee landowner who spent most of his time in Sussex, consulted Rev. Adam Sedgwick, the Woodwardian Professor of Geology and curator of Cambridge University's Museum of Geology.

> "Mr. Headly of Cambridge has it seems embarked in a somewhat extensive "Coprolite" Speculation and has asked permission to prosecute his search for this fossil matter upon my Property in the village of Haslingfield near Cambridge. Before I enter into any treaty with Mr. H. - who however offers what appears to be reasonable terms - I should esteem it a very great favour if you give me your opinion generally as to the probabilities of such a project being other than purely visionary - like so many others of the present day."
>
> (CUL. Add.7652 II/C/4)

Although Sedgwick's opinion has not come to light, it probably advised the Earl to allow Headly access and realise the vast financial potential of having his land worked. The 4th Earl of Hardwicke, Queen Victoria's Lord-in-Waiting, was reported to have made £5,000 a year from coprolite royalties on his Wimpole estate. The 5th earl inherited the fortune and his nephew claimed that it was squandered on drinking, horses and gambling. This earned him the nickname "Champagne Charlie". (CUL. Palmer Papers B51, Yorke, A.C. (1979), 'Wimpole as I knew it', p.12)

De la Warr's arrangements with Headly have not come to light but workings were soon established in the area. Mr Levi was taken on as Headly's coprolite foreman and a gang of diggers was engaged. Some may well have been local farmers' agricultural labourers but experienced diggers from other workings are known to have moved into parishes where the seam was found. Diggers from Suffolk moved into the area and there are reports that gangs of Irish labour were involved. Fascinating insight into the effect that these gangs had on the area was recorded in an account of the life story of Annie Macpherson. She moved into Little Eversden in 1858 with her parents to stay with their aunt.

> "Just at this time the discovery was made that the fossils embedded in the clay soil of that neighbourhood formed, when ground to powder, a valuable manure for the land. Within a week about 500 rough miners and labourers poured into the quiet little villages, and the pressing need was felt of efforts to civilise and evangelise these men, not only for their own sakes, but to save the rustics of the villages from the contamination brought about by the drunken and loose habits of these invaders of their peace, and the immorality induced by the absence of any provision for lodging and sleeping accommodation for this unprecedented addition to the countryside".

(Birt, Lilian (1931), 'The Children's Home Finder', pp.9-14)

The impact that the diggers had on the local community will be examined in more detail later. Coprolite diggers were easy to notice out in the fields. Enid Porter was told that they wore thick union flannel shirts, fustian trousers tied with "lalley gags", a fustian jacket and the inevitable red handkerchief. To keep the rain off their heads and the sun out of their eyes they wore a black cap with a patent leather peak. On their feet they wore fen-type boots with two or three tongues which reached four inches above the ankle. To give them a better grip in the bottom of the pit they fastened iron creepers to their boots. Iron insteps helped to prevent the boot from wearing away with the regular spadework. These would have been locked up in the shed after they finished work rather than carry them home. (Porter, E. Notes in Cambridge Folk Museum on her conversation with C. A. Swann; Examples can be seen in Ashwell Museum)

Whether Levi took on some of the agricultural labourers working on De la Warr's land or brought in a gang of labourers from outside the parish is not known. Often the contract was for several years so any newcomers needed accommodation, food and entertainment. Opportunities to capitalise on this demand were not lost on some local entrepreneurs. As shall be seen, the coprolite diggers were not welcomed by all sections of the village.

Further agreements might have been won from De La Warr or from neighbouring landowners but few of these records have not come to light. Much of the evidence that has been found tends to be based on the correspondence and solicitor's agreements of the larger landowners which has been deposited in the Record Office. Smaller landowners' records have mostly been destroyed. In 1860 Charles Bidwell reported on a survey he carried out in Harston on the 260-acre farm and six cottages belonging to the Beldam Estate. The tenant was Mrs Watson, a widow, whose rent was £418. Bidwell noted that it was *"badly distributed...* (and) *contains in many parts coprolites".* Although no evidence has emerged to show that Bedlam then arranged to have them raised, it is most likely they would have been. (CCRO. R57.8.24) One of the first people recorded as exploiting the Harston coprolites at this time was Charles Gilbey. He was an insurance agent living at 11 Church Street. Like many others at that time who had available capital, he speculated in the coprolite business and may even have had arrangements with the Beldams.

Census returns, local newspapers and Kelly's Post Office Directory included reference to the industry. In Kelly's 1861 edition its description of Haslingfield added that

> "In this parish and neighbourhood fossils are found in abundance, they are known by the name of coprolites, and have become of great importance to agriculturalists".

(Kelly's Post Office Directory,1861)

The 1861 census showed Hauxton's population had dropped 16% to 262 and there was no evidence that anyone was involved in the diggings.. Trumpington's population had increased every decade during the first half of the century but dropped 7% to 716. Could some of them have been attracted by demand for labour in the coprolite diggings in other parishes? 33-year old James Smith, of 18 London Road, was described as *"foreman of the coprolite diggers."* Which diggers one asks? Did he manage one of the diggings on Coldham's Lane, on Newmarket Road, in Chesterton or were there pits in Trumpington? There was no mention in the census of anyone else being involved. That is not to say that there were none. In cases where farmers employed their own labourers to do the digging they could still have described it as "agricultural labour". Smith was from Suffolk where the diggings first started. Did he move into the area when the industry started here? Could he have been related to William Cross Smith, a Chemist and Druggist of Fitzroy Street, Cambridge who had won a licence to work them on Coldham's Lane.

There was a similar decline in Cambridge's population over the decade. It dropped by 289 to 30,797. Maybe the Duke of Manchester's recruitment officers had successfully taken on some of the local men to fight in his regiment in the Crimean War? Maybe men and boys had joined the coprolite gangs in the fenland and other workings? However, fifteen men were involved in the diggings in the city. Analysis of their home locations gives one an impression of how widespread the work was. There were six men from Holy Trinity parish and three from St. Giles, including 42-year old Philip Dale, the Foreman of the Coprolite Works. He lived at Warren's Passage. Two men came from Carter's Yard, off Castle Street, and in St. Peter's parish, one man lived on Northampton Street and another in the Spotted Cow Yard. Only four came from St. Andrew the Less, 40-year old John Thomas Hunt, the Inspector of Coprolites, two more diggers and Alfred Walton, an engine driver at the Walton's Bone Manure Factory.

34-year old Nathaniel Warren Johnson was living in St. George's Terrace. He was Packard's agent. His entry revealed the domination of the industry by the Eastern Counties Manure Company as he was described as a

> "Coprolite Merchant and tenant farmer holding about 13 acres employing 8 men and 5 boys. Raising of Coprolite the undersigned employs about 375 men and boys in various parts of Cambridgeshire."
>
> (CCRO 1861 census)

Coming from Suffolk he must have recruited experienced diggers as a number of Suffolk villages reported declining populations owing to the labourers migrating to Cambridgeshire, *"where more available deposits have been discovered."* (Suffolk County Record Office, 1861 census)

Grantchester's population increased by eleven over the decade to 696. It did not appear to have had the dramatic influx of labourers as in other parishes. This suggests it was mainly farmers employing their own labourers. There were twelve gardeners, ten millers and six farmers. Twenty men and boys were described as *"Coperlite labourers"* in the village. This gives more an indication of local accent than the poor spelling of the census enumerator. Whilst the census was taken in April it may have been that at that time the men were needed on agricultural work and so many did not describe the work as coprolite labour. There were sixty-five working as agricultural labourers and forty-six *"labourers"*, any number of whom could have been involved. This would bring the numbers up to sixty-six, just under 10% of the population! The average age of those described as involved was 27 but the most were in their late teens and early twenties. The eldest was 67 and the youngest 11. Four, all from Gamlingay, were lodgers at Wright's Farm. This suggests that they may have been working pits there but documentation for this has not emerged. Interestingly, only 60% of them were born in the parish, which confirms the influx of migrant workers to the diggings.

There had only been an increase of twelve over the decade in Harston to give a population of 782. This suggests that those involved must have described themselves as farm labourers or simply labourers. 66-year old Joseph Ellis was described as a "Fossil Merchant" living on the High Street. He may well have been responsible for arranging the sale of the coprolites to manure manufacturers. No other records of his involvement have come to light. (CCRO. 1861 census)

By spring 1861 Gilbey must have realised the deposit extended onto land belonging to Jesus College. On 3rd February he signed a lease allowing him three acres of their 206-acre Rectory Farm. In those days it was known as Impropiah Farm. The map on page ... shows it was in the 16a.3r.7p. field, immediately to the west of the farmhouse. (OS. 426523) He agreed to work the deposit down to twelve feet (3.7m.) paying a royalty of £70 per acre and to compensate the tenant farmer, William Long, whilst the field was "*out of cultivation*". (Jesus College Mun. Harston.) He would have engaged a gang of men, possibly Long's farm labourers, and they would have set to work in removing the topsoil and then working down through the subsoil to reach the fossil seam. A washmill to clean the fossils was erected by the farm using water from a nearby pump. After sorting, a great pile of them would have accumulated by the farm track, ready to be carted to the Cambridge Road and on to Harston Station.

A short account of the work was included in Rev. G. Davis' account of Haslingfield's history. He confirmed that the deposit was one of the earliest in the area to be extracted on account of their shallow depth.

> "When the coprolites lay within a short distance of the surface, and so easier and cheaper to work, they were said to lay fleet. They were never found quite at or near the surface... thick mud when washed off was used for levelling the land and sometimes for brickmaking".
>
> (.Davis, Rev. G.E 'History of Haslingfield,' pp.31-2.)

Brick, tile and pipe making was a common industry on the Gault clay in this area. Following the Parish Enclosure Act, farmers were keen to use the newly mass-produced pipes to improve the poorly drained clay fields. Records show that William Coxall, a Haslingfield farmer, had purchased 6,000 drainage tiles to drain his 250-acre farm at "Bottom Lane" in 1861. According to the census it was only a small scale operation as he employed nine labourers and three boys. The trenching work must have exposed the coprolite seam in his fields where it outcropped in the Greensand between the gault clay and the chalk marl down by the river. Later evidence suggests he similarly capitalised on the work, no doubt using his own labourers instead of having an outside contractor do the work. The Coxall family became quite involved in the industry as a Daniel Coxall was at different times foreman of both the Haslingfield and Harston fossil works and James Coxall was a beerhouse keeper, quite possibly providing ale for the hard working diggers. (CCRO.1861 census; R59/27/1/2)

Where the coprolites were sold remains unknown as nothing of Gilbey's or Coxall's accounts or correspondence has come to light. Given Headly's involvement he might well have purchased them. Three acres was not a large scale operation and the bursar of Jesus College would have been keen to

Lower Cretaceous Terrestrial Communities
a *Iguanadon* (Vertebrata: Reptilia: Archosaur – dinosaur)
b *Megalosaurus* (Vertebrata: Reptilia: Archosaur – dinosaur)
c *Hypsilophodon* (Vertebrata: Reptilia: Archosaur – dinosaur)
d *Acanthopholis* (Vertebrata: Reptilia: Archosaur – dinosaur)
e *Equisetites* (Pteridophyta: Calamites – horsetails)

(McKerrow, W.S.. (1978), *The Ecology of Fossils: An Illustrated Guide*, Duckworth, p.297)

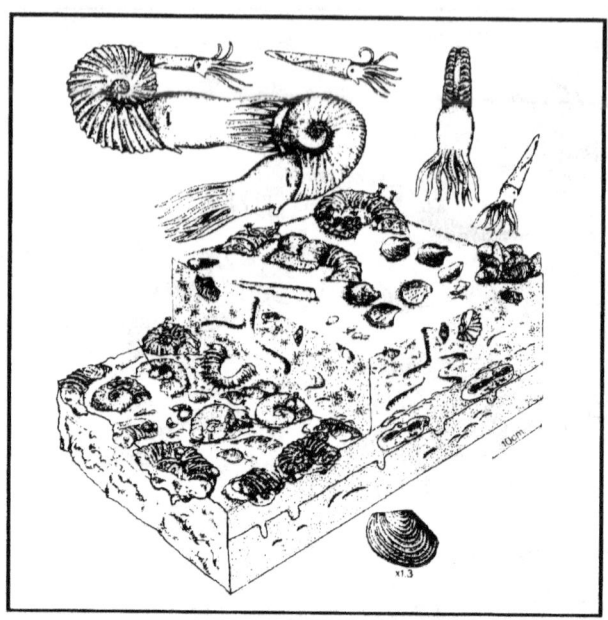

The Phosphate bed Community
(McKerrow, W.S.. (1978), *The Ecology of Fossils: An Illustrated Guide*,
Duckworth, p.286)

Cambridgeshire coprolites. (Photograph courtesy of Earth
Sciences Museum, Cambridge)

Cambridgeshire coprolites, thought to be 170 million years old. (Courtesy of Tim Gane)

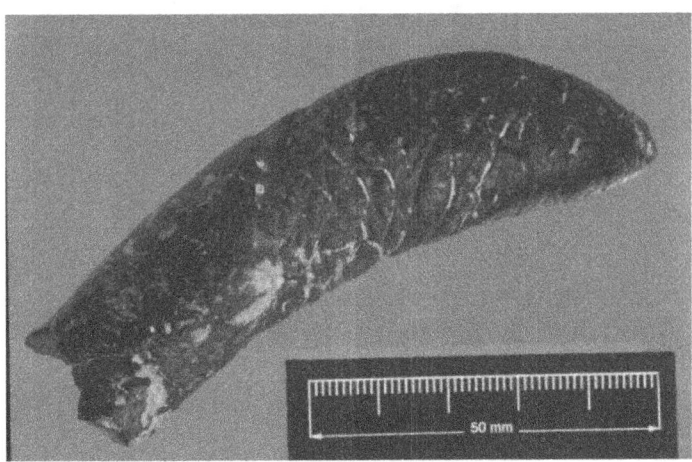

The Barrington coprolite
(Photograph courtesy of Earth Sciences Museum, Cambridge)

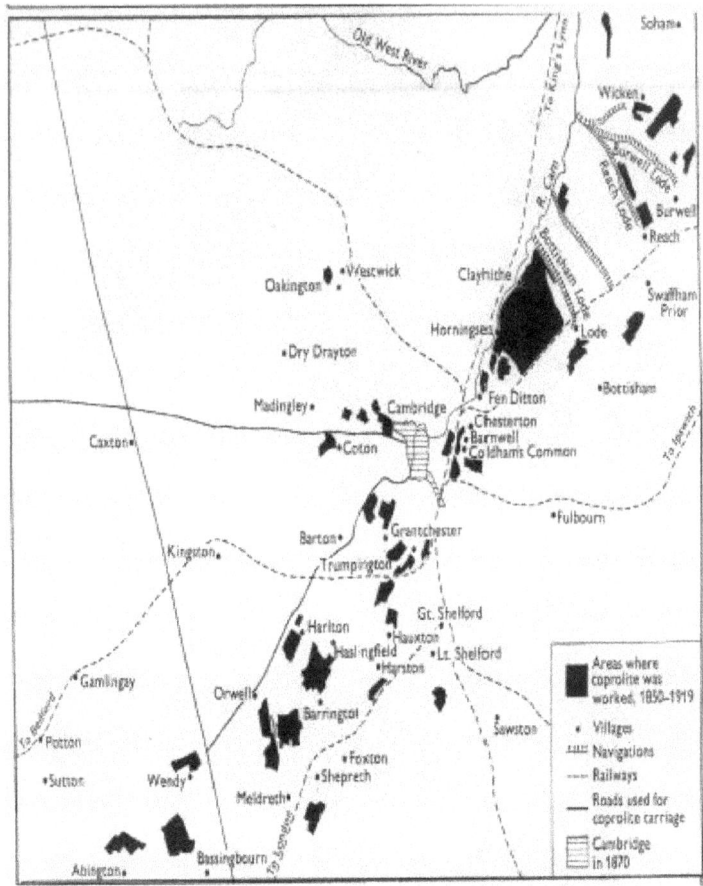

The extent of the coprolite diggings across Cambridgeshire
(Grove, R. (1976), The Cambridgeshire Coprolite Mining Rush,
Oleander Press)

The Hauxton Fossil Diggings

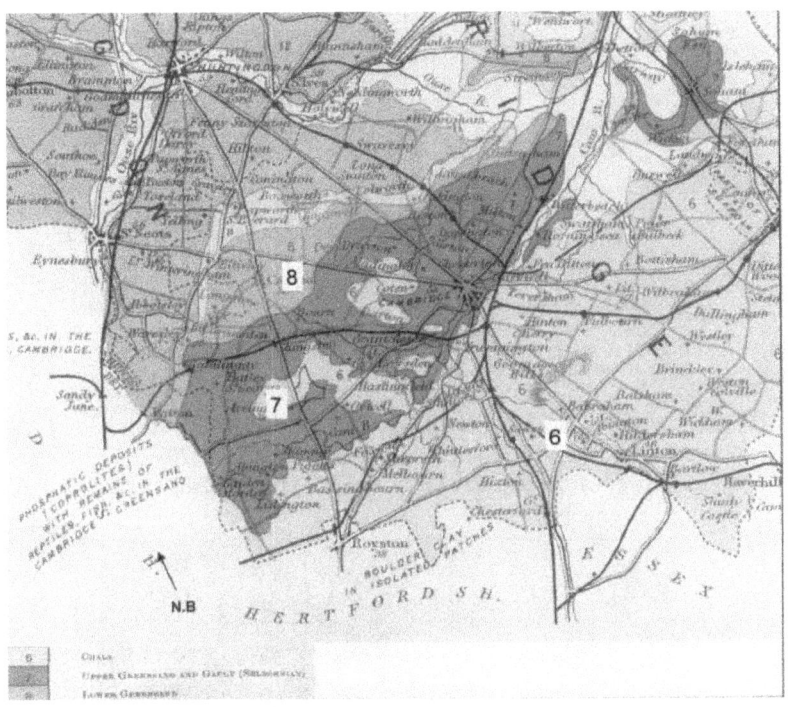

Extract from geological map of southwest Cambridgeshire after Woodward (1904 based on Reynolds (Ian West 2001)
6 = Chalk; 7 = Upper Greensand; 8 = Lower Greensand

Coprolite Diggings at Orwell, Cambridgeshire. 1860s – 1870s
(Courtesy of Cambridgeshire Collection W27.1J80 25358)

Coprolite Diggings in Cow Pasture, Abington Pigotts, Cambridgeshire, 1883
(Courtesy of Mr and Mrs Sclater, Abington Pigotts)

The Hauxton Fossil Diggings

Steam engine hauling coprolites from Whaddon to Shepreth Station c.1880
(Cambridge Collection Q AR J8 11029 Courtesy of Mrs Coningsby, Whaddon)

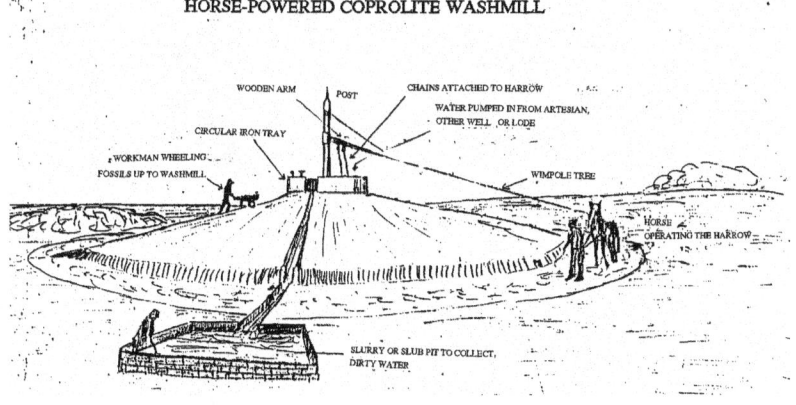

(Based on sketch in Richard Grove's Cambridgeshire Coprolite Mining Rush)

Undated photograph of a circular coprolite harrow
Cambridgeshire Collection: W27.1. KO. 19554).

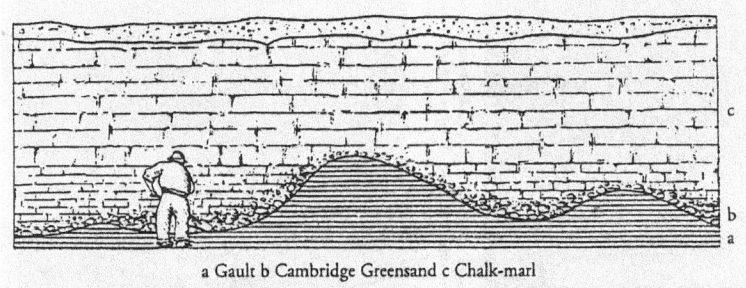

a Gault b Cambridge Greensand c Chalk-marl

View of a coprolite pit in Horningsea, Cambs.
(Jukes-Browne, A.J. & Hill, W. *Cretaceous Rocks of Britain,* Mem. Geol. Surv.
1903, p.194)

The Hauxton Fossil Diggings

Undated photograph of coprolite diggers in Orwell, Cambridgeshire
(Courtesy of Sue Miller, Orwell History Society)

Undated postcard of horse-drawn tumbrils carrying coprolites to the railway station at Millbrook, Bedfordshire.

Photographs of the coprolite works on Sandy Heath, Bedfordshire, c.1882) The top photo shows women outside the sorting shed. The lower photographs shows a horse-powered cylindrical washmill.
(Courtesy of Potton History Society)

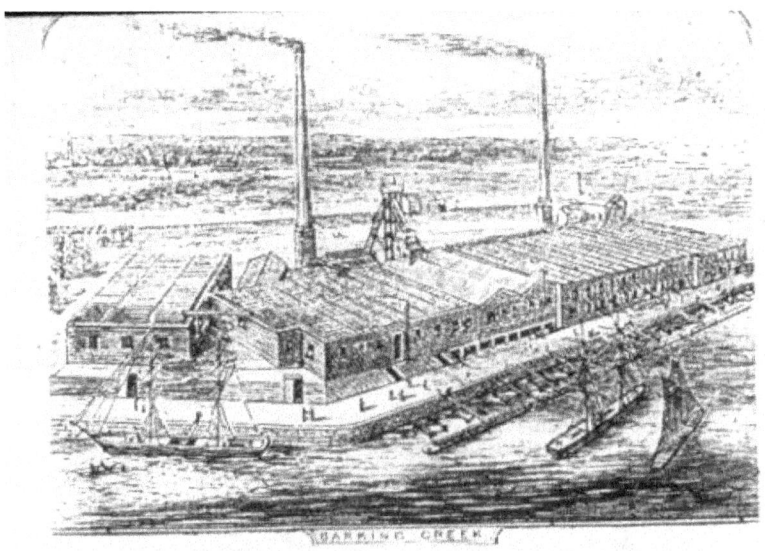

Lawes Chemical Manure Company works at Deptford Creek, established in 1857, 15 years after Lawes opened his works in Barking (Courtesy of Lawes Agricultural Trust, Rothamsted Agricultural Station)

Undated photograph of coprolites being unloaded from lighters at Lawes Chemical Manure Company works (Courtesy of Lawes Agricultural Trust, Rothamsted Agricultural Station)

Caricature of J.B. Lawes who patented the technique of dissolving coprolite and other phosphatic materials in sulphuric acid to produce superphosphate. He set up his own manure company, won contracts to raise coprolites and purchased others from diggings across south-east England (*Vanity Fair* 8th July 1882)

Undated photograph of Edward Packard (1819 – 1899) who founded Edward Packard and Company. In 1843 he began making superphosphate by dissolving old bones in sulphuric acid at Snape Mill. In 1851 he built Britain's first complete sulphuric acid and superphosphate works at Bramford and went on to win coprolite agreements and purchase coprolites from across southeast England.
(http://www.yara.com/en/about/yara_centennial/heritage/fisons_inter.html)

discover more on the property, given that agricultural rents were seldom more than thirty shillings (£1.50) an acre. Later that year Charles Bidwell was asked to survey the farm. His report to the bursar suggested it worth twenty-eight shillings

1861 photograph of William Colchester (1813–1898), one of the first manure manufacturers to use Suffolk coprolites. Had manure works in Ipswich, moved into Cambridgeshire fens in 1846, won coprolite contracts and purchased others from diggings across southeast England.
(Courtesy of Giles Colchester)

The Hauxton Fossil Diggings

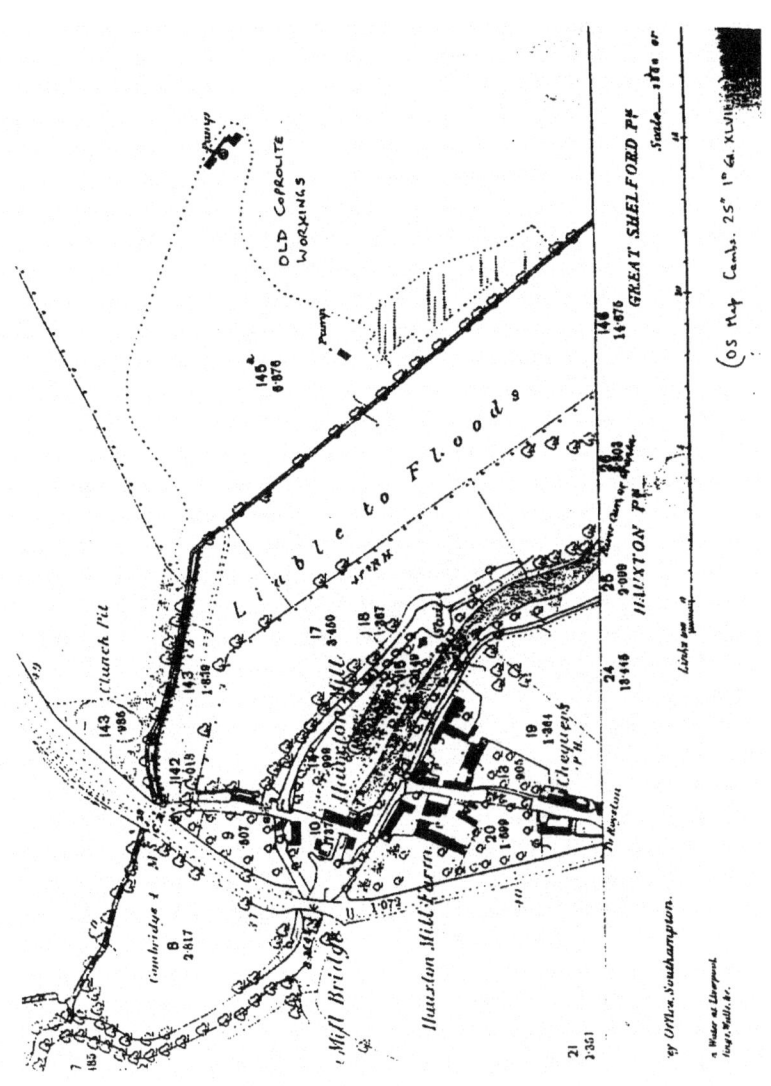

King's College, Cambridge
Coprolite land at Grantchester dug by Mr F. Lilley and W.E. Lilley 1865 - 1885

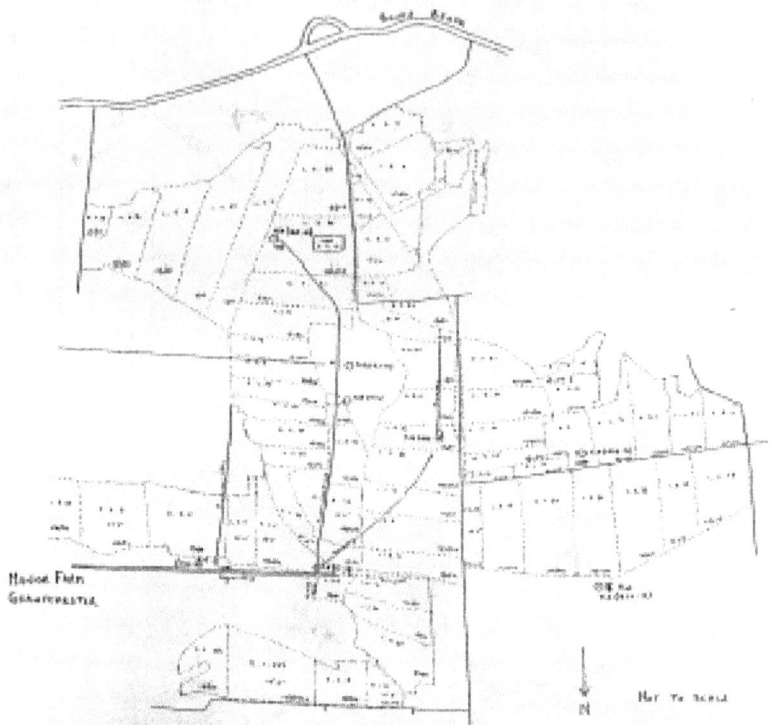

(King's College Archive - Gra/818)

King's College, Cambridge
Coprolite Land at Grantchester
Dug by Mr. H. Banyard 1866 - 71

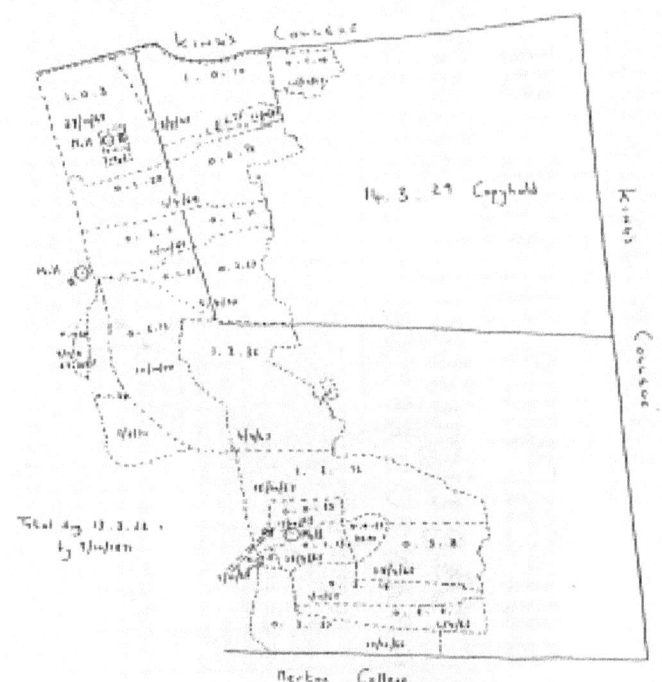

(King's Coll. Gm/822)

EDWARD ABRAHALL,
Manufacturer of the STANDARD
SUPERPHOSPHATE OF LIME,
AND OTHER
Agricultural Manures,
GRANTCHESTER, NEAR CAMBRIDGE.

SUPERPHOSPHATE OF LIME is made by the action of Sulphuric Acid on bones. The Phosphate is rendered soluble by the acid, so that the young plants can, from the first, obtain the ingredients essential to their growth. The turnip is thus brought rapidly past the fly, and is ready for the hoe in a very short space of time. A much smaller amount of this manure than of bones is required to produce the same result. From 3 to 4 cwt. should be used per acre, adding double the weight of ashes to be thoroughly mixed and drilled in with the seed. Price £5½ per ton.

CORN MANURES,
Particularly suitable for WHEAT, OATS, BEANS, PEAS, TARES, MANGOLD, and BARLEY. These Manures contain fertilising properties in the best form for giving strength and affording nourishment to the plant throughout its entire progress, greatly tending to the development of the grain. Note—these Manures being highly charged with Ammonia, they must not be allowed to come in direct contact with the seed. From 4 to 5 cwt. per acre sown broadcast before or after the drill, and harrowed in. price £4 10s.

Bags charged for. Half-price allowed, if returned in good condition.

Cassey's Directory of Cambridgeshire, 1864

Steam plough preparing the ground for the Hauxton Road coprolite works during the First World War (Courtesy of Henry Boot and Son)

The Hauxton Fossil Diggings

Steam-powered shovel on the Hauxton Road Coprolite works (Courtesy of Henry Boot Securing the railtrack at the Hauxton Road Coprolite works (Courtesy of Henry Boot and Son and The Cambridge Collection, 93/31/2)

Securing the railtrack at the Hauxton Road Coprolite works (Courtesy of Henry Boot and Son and The Cambridge Collection, 93/31/2)

Steam-powered Lubecker excavator and drag line used in WW1 Trumpington Coprolite works (Courtesy of Henry Boot and Son and The Cambridge Collection,93/31/18)

Dragline excavating the trench (Courtesy of Henry Boot and Son and The Cambridge Collection,93/31/17)

Trench cut to expose coprolite bed (Courtesy of Henry Boot and Son and The Cambridge Collection,93/Railway and workmen in the coprolite trench (Courtesy of Henry Boot and Son and The Cambridge Collection,93/31/14)

Railway and workmen in the coprolite trench (Courtesy of Henry Boot and Son and The Cambridge Collection,93/31/14)

Steam-powered excavator (Courtesy of Henry Boot and Son and The Cambridge Collection, 93/31/19)

Irish 'prisoners-of-war' digging out coprolite (Courtesy of Henry Boot and Son and The Cambridge Collection, 93/31/2)

The Hauxton Fossil Diggings

Railway crane hauling coprolite into trucks (Courtesy of Henry Boot and Son and The Cambridge Collection 93/13/1)

Railtrack on top of embankment (Courtesy of Henry Boot and Son and The Cambridge Collection, 93/13/16)

Steam crane at coprolite works (Courtesy of Henry Boot and Son and The Cambridge Collection, 93/13/11)

Coprolite washing station at Trumpington (Courtesy of Henry Boot and Son and The Cambridge Collection, 93/13/13)

Electric motor in the coprolite washing station (Courtesy of Henry Boot and Son and The Cambridge Collection, 93/13/?)

Electric motor in the coprolite washing station (Courtesy of Henry Boot and Son and The Cambridge Collection, 93/13/?)

Cylindrical coprolite washer, Trumpington (Courtesy of Henry Boot and Son and The Cambridge Collection, 93/13/15)

Lines of slurry leading from coprolite washing station (Courtesy of Henry Boot and Son and The Cambridge Collection, 93/13/14)

The Hauxton Fossil Diggings

Slurry pits at Trumpington (Courtesy of Henry Boot and Son and The Cambridge Collection,, 93/13/13)

Hauxton Road Coprolite works from top of embankment Courtesy of Henry Boot and Son and The Cambridge Collection,, 93/13/?)

Steam train and drop-sided coprolite trucks (Courtesy of Henry Boot and Son and The Cambridge Collection,, 93/13/?)

Buildings associated with Hauxton Road Coprolite works (Courtesy of Henry Boot and Son and The Cambridge Collection,, 93/13/?)

Sale No. 2879.

G. R.
MINISTRY OF MUNITIONS.
By direction of the Surplus Government Property Disposal Board (Machinery & Plant Section).

HAUXTON ROAD, TRUMPINGTON, and GRANTCHESTER, Cambs.
(About 3½ miles from Cambridge Station).

Catalogue of the Valuable

MACHINERY & PLANT
Of the Coprolite Workings

At above, including :

4 Lubecker Excavators and 5 Conveyors
8 Coprolite Washing Mills, 22 Steam Pumps, 2 Lister Petrol Engines with Pumps,
4 Powerful Steam Navvies
5 Boiler Shells, 4 Vertical Boilers, 4 Hind & Lund's Grinders and 4 Amalgamators,
9 Steam Travelling and Derrick Cranes
3 Crab Winches, Weston Chain Blocks, Hydraulic, Bottle and Traversing Jacks,
2 0—6—0 and 2 0—4—0 Type Locomotives
390 Tons of Rails, Large Quantity of Clyde Dogs, Fishplates, and Fang Bolts,
2 Powerful Gas Engines
2 Crossley's Oil Engines, 4 Portable Engines and Boilers, 3 Screw Cutting Lathes, Shaping, Punching, Shearing, Planing and Thicknessing Machines,
2 Electric Generating Plants
20 Compound and Shunt Wound Motors, 9,000 Yards of Cable, Electrical Spares,
2 Suction Gas Producing Plants
Large Quantity of Water and Steam Pipe, Sluice Valves, 60 Tons of Piling Monkeys,
Consumable Stores and Spares
Tool Steel, Flat Steel, 15 Tons of Bolts and Rivets,
115 Standards of Timber
26 Jubilee Tip Wagons, Portable Forges, Anvils, Stocks and Dies, 19 Canadian Slip Scrapers,
33 Timber Built Huts
Principally Sectional, 3-Ton Austin Lorry, Ford Touring Car, Cadillac 30—40 H.P. Touring Car, 2-Ton Dray, 4-Wheeled Water Cart, and numerous Miscellaneous Effects,

which Messrs.

CATLING & SON

Are instructed to Sell by Auction, at the Workings as above, on

TUESDAY, November 25, 1919, and Four Following Days

The above may be viewed any Day prior to Sale, and Catalogues obtained of the Auctioneers, 6, St. Andrew's Street, Cambridge. Tel. 366.

NOTE.—"SURPLUS," price 3d., the Official List of Government Property for Sale, published Twice Monthly, on Sale Everywhere.

Printed by Fabb & Tyler, Ltd., Cambridge.

Sale particulars of Trumpington Coprolite works, National Archives Mun.4.6330 pp.23,37)

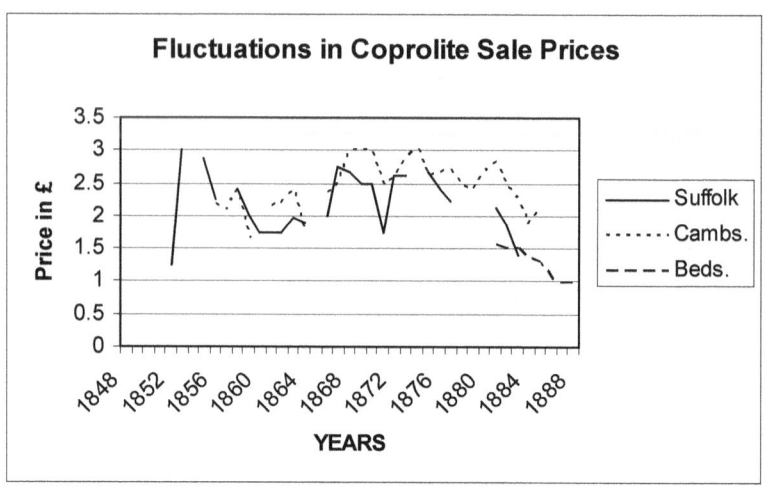

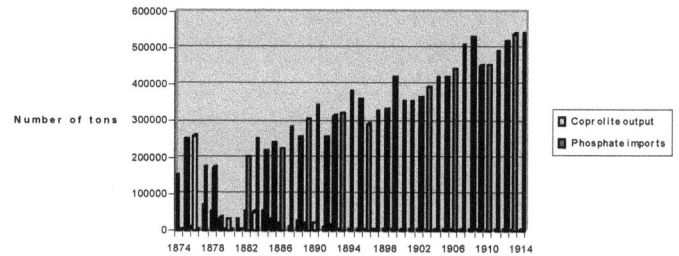

(£1.40) an acre and *"of good quality, a portion about 3 acres contains coprolites in No.6 has been let to raise at £70 per acre"*. (CCRO. Bidwell,19, p.5)

Documents show that Gilbey and Headly made other arrangements with landowners of adjoining fields and exploited further deposits. Gilbey must have been well liked by his employees as, a few years later, the Cambridge Chronicle reported on: -

__Harston Labourer's Treat__. - Mr. Gilbey, master of the Harston fossil pits, gave all his labourers (about 30 in number) a treat of a real old English supper, on Friday the 29th of January at the "Old English Gentleman". After the labourers' supper Mr. Gilbey entertained several of his friends. The Harston Brass band was in attendance, and played in good style for the enjoyment of the party. The supper was served by Mr and Mrs Whitehead, the host and hostess, and gave great satisfaction to all parties."

(Cambridge Chronicle 6th February 1864 p.8)

A few other examples of local employers providing similar entertainment for their labourers can be seen later. By June 1864 Gilbey's men had worked 5a.1r.0p. which meant he must have paid Jesus College about £370, the equivalent value of a small estate. Bidwell informed the bursar that *"he has levelled the land and left it satisfactory to W. Long"*. His map can be seen on page ... Further correspondence showed that, in order to facilitate the transport of the coprolites, he was then allowed to construct a tramway from the pit to the Harston Road *"so as not to injure the private road"*. (Jesus College, Muniments Harston) Headly, who was later to take on the working of Haslingfield Charity Farm, had his tramway leading across the river, past these workings and onto the main road.

When the yield was up to 300 tons an acre and selling price up to sixty shillings (£3.00) a ton in the mid-1860s, the coprolite contractors' financial success was secured. Before costs Gilbey was making several thousand pounds. This encouraged Mason Moses in Haslingfield to get involved. In the village directory of 1864 he advertised as *"grocer, draper, coprolite contractor and merchant"*. (Cassey's 1864 directory) He must have been engaged in working deposits on other landowners' fields and arranged their sale to the manure manufacturers. Their demand for the coprolites was rising throughout this period.

Moses was considered an astute but totally mean employer who had purchased land from Haslingfield Charity. Whether it was also dug for coprolites is undocumented. On his long stretch of land fronting onto the High Street he had his house, shop and butchery built. Knowing the demand from the diggers for accommodation he erected six brick-fronted and clunch-backed cottages facing the High Street each with butter kitchens and lean-tos as well as eight clunch cottages on the Back Lane. These were poor quality cottages with simple kitchens, earth floors, two rooms upstairs and a small piece of land outside where the tenants could grow vegetables, keep poultry and a pig. He insisted that the fourteen occupiers were "diggers" and arranged that all their grocery requirements were provided at his shop with their rent and bills deducted from the weekly wages he gave them. There was gossip that they even had to order their fish from his wife who would add a few pennies to the cost and she used to sell the villagers some of the best pears around for two pennies, far more than their real worth. Although Moses gave a small plot of land to the village for a chapel it reportedly had no land around it and there was not even a right of way. (Communication with Mrs Wilshere,

Haslingfield, who in 1990 lived in Mason's "Town House". She was told this story as a child by children of the coprolite diggers.)

Over in Harlton the diggings had also started in the 1850s. There were deposits found in the 2a.1r.0p. field belonging to the Red Lion Public House. (CUL. PSQ.18.498) There must have been an expansion of the diggings by the mid-1860s as in October 1865 the Cambridge Chronicle reported

"HARLTON. Accident - On Wednesday, William Clark, a coprolite digger, met with an accident in this village. He was at work when a quantity of earth fell on him and fractured his thigh-bone. He was taken to Addenbrooke's Hospital, Cambridge, and is now getting on towards recovery."

(Cambridge Chronicle 7th October 1865 p.8)

The first evidence of any formal agreement in Harlton was not until 1867. In the October of 1866 a Mr. Whitechurch had taken on a thirteen-year lease of a farm in the parish. He must have suspected the coprolite seam was to be found under some of the fields. The Cambridge solicitor, Clement Francis, was called in and he prepared instructions to invite most of the big names in the coprolite industry in Cambridgeshire to test the land. They included John Bennet Lawes, William Colchester and Edward Packard as well as local coprolite contractors, Messrs. Coxall, Heffer, Carver, Griffin, Wallis and Roads. Only Wallis and Packard were prepared to test the land and it was Packard's manager, Nathaniel Johnson, who reported to Francis the bad news. There were no coprolites within a depth of about twenty-one feet except in about one acre in the corner of the field. (CCRO. Francis Bill Books 1867 p.267-268) Whether Mr. Whitechurch got the licence as sitting tenant is not known.

It must have become clear that the eastward development of the diggings in nearby Barrington indicated that Haslingfield Charity Farm similarly had this fossil deposit beneath it. This was land that had been left to Haslingfield parish by Richard Skelman. The trustees, aware of potentially huge fortune to be made, arranged to have the land tested. The Chairman at this time was William Coxall who in May 1867 arranged with Trinity College to raise the coprolites from one of their fields. (CCRO. Francis Bill Books 1867 p.138) Coxall must have appreciated the potential of this find and the secretary confirmed it. It was put forward that, once in operation, the coprolite workings would alleviate the employment situation in the village by providing work for the poor and "vagrants" on parish relief. They also considered that the revenue from leasing the coprolite land would help reduce the gentry's contribution to the parish Poor Rate. (Grove, R. (1976), 'The Cambridgeshire Coprolite Mining Rush', p.42) The surveyors, Mann and Raven, were called in who duly sent the following report:-

Mann & Raven, Land Agents,
June 18th 1867
Cambridge.

Charity Farm, Haslingfield, occupied by Mr. Lunnis.

We have examined the lands in the occupation of Mr. Lunnis and find that there are from thirteen to fourteen acres which contain coprolite, in different parts of the farm, from 10 to 14 feet from surface. There are about three acres lying in the pasture and fields adjoining, the working of which would not interfere injuriously with the rest of the Arable land. This might be commenced immediately after harvest. If an arrangement can be arrived at with the present tenant we should advise that the farm and coprolite should be let by tender in one lot.

(CCRO.R59/27/1/3)

The fields shown to contain a workable deposit were marked on the tithe map as Nos. 251, 253-4, 254a, 255-7. They were valued by Mr. Lunnis for farming as correspondence shows he was not keen on the idea of forfeiting his lease on the farm without adequate compensation. With coprolite contractors willing to pay well over £100 an acre, the committee wanted to act quickly on the surveyor's advice. They resolved that

> "...the secretary be authorised in the second week of September next to request tenders to be sent for raising coprolites by Messrs. Packard, Jarvis of Cambridge, William Wallis of Harston, Headley of Cambridge, Colchester of Ipswich and William Reynolds of Coton, the contracting parties making all necessary arrangements for compensating the occupier of the lands."

(CCRO. R59/27/5/1)

In the meantime another contractor appeared on the scene, Robert Mason of Reach. In the December of 1868, he agreed to work part of Queen's College land in Haslingfield farmed by Mr. Hall. He paid them a royalty of £135 per acre but for only two roods. (CCRO. Bidwell's diary, 12th Dec.1868) It was not until February 1869, however, that the trustees of Charity Farm came up with a solution. They included the vicar, Rev. George Clements, Orwell's rector, Rev. H.C.A. Tayler (who had his own coprolite account from Trinity College for the coprolites raised on Orwell's glebe land), Earl De La Warr, John Sergeant, W. Coleman Wallis, Henry Hurrell and W.W. Wallis. It was decided to sell the coprolites to Richard Jarvis. The deeds show him to have been a *"Coprolite Merchant and Mineral Agent,"* of 46 Russell St., Cambridge. He was prepared to pay them £120 per acre but Lunnis adamantly refused to being removed from the farm. The trustees compromised and instead agreed

> "to sell copralites [sic] on the south side of the Barton Road Call [sic] Clay pits for £45 to Mr. Jarvis, he to compensate the tenant 64 poles or less".
>
> (CCRO. R59/27/5/1)

Jarvis must have taken on a gang of labourers to prepare the land by digging up obstacles like trees, removing the topsoil and subsoil and erecting a washmill where the fossils were to be cleaned. By July he had paid the committee £103.50, not quite an acre's royalty, but apparently he still had not struck a suitable bargain with Lunnis over compensation.

In May 1868, James Jarvis, a Cambridge coprolite merchant and probably a relative of Richard Jarvis, won a licence to raise them from the 4a.3r.4p. field belonging to St. Catherine's College beside the Haslingfield parish boundary. He may have been involved in the earlier works. He paid them £125 per acre, nearly double Gilbey's royalty, and was given permission to erect a washmill and sink a well for the works. The college stipulated that he had to have the work completed by Michaelmas the next year. (St. Catherine's Coll. Mun; Whitaker, W. 'Water Supply of Cambs.' Mem. Geol. Surv. London, 1921, p.74) Jarvis, it appeared, found this schedule "too tight" and the college's surveyor reported,

> "...he said he could not undertake to do so as the slurry and deposit might not be sufficiently dry. However if the land is not finished by Autumn 1869 it will be ready to sow with a spring crop and it is better to wait until the land is thoroughly dry in the autumn before it is levelled".

(St. Cath's. College Mun. XXX/4.)

In the June of 1868, on one of Bidwell's many visits to College farms in the area, he met Jarvis at Harlton with the vicar, Rev. York. A verbal agreement was made whereby he agreed he work an acre of Mr. Prime's Farm at £80. If the seam was good, he would pay £90, quite a reasonable agreement in the circumstances. (CCRO. Bidwell's diary May 1868 diary) In November St. Catherine's College allowed him a further three roods at £110 so he was well supplied with work. This explained why, the next year, he was very keen to rent a small homestead and land in Harlton from the college. (St. Cath's Mun. Harlton XXX/4) He must have been engaged in work on other property as the college accounts for Harlton only revealed sums of £78, £63, £45, and £90 for the four years from 1868. Although this was very little compared to some of the colleges they used some of this coprolite revenue on "permanent improvements" to their property in the parish. (CUL.Rep.Com. Univ. Income (C. 856-11) p256, HC 1873 xxxvii.3)

Another major landowner in the area was Edward Humphreys Greene de Freville of Hinxton Hall. He owned land adjacent to Gilbey's fossil pits in Harston. According to the evidence, on the 20th October 1866, he gave a licence to John Watson, a local Harston farmer *"to excavate, search for, get and carry away the mineral or substance known as coprollate"* (sic). "Coprollate" must have been the local accent. Watson agreed to pay £160 per acre, one of the highest rates in this area of the "coprolite belt". He was given the right to two acres of land tenanted by Lydia Watson, presumably his relative. There must have been some concern over the conduct of the coprolite labourers as, according to the local historian, Richard Grove "strict provisions were imposed on them". (CCRO.1860 R51/24/27/1; Grove, R. (1976), 'The Cambridgeshire

Coprolite Mining Rush', Oleander Press, p.14.)

In the May of 1868, given the success of his neighbouring farmers, John Whitechurch, the tenant of the 308a.0r.26p. Harlton Manor Farm, on taking over his father's lease, gained a licence from the landlords, Christ's Hospital, London to raise the fossils. He was allowed to work fifteen acres *"near the house and buildings"* paying £90 per acre and agreeing to work down to thirteen feet until 1871. (Guildhall Library, London, Christ's Hospital, Court Minute Book, Vol.17,p559) The agreement stipulated he work only two acres at a time and

"...at his own cost to level the whole of the ground worked, and restore the surface after the digging, and to seed it down again in permanent pasture."

(Ibid.)

The financial success of the coprolite works led parish overseers and churchwardens to consider including them in the Poor's Rate. In November 1868 the Court of the Queens Bench (under 12 and 13 Vict.,cap.45,see.11.) decided they should be because of the increased value of the land. This rate was a kind of tax on local businesses to raise funds to help the poor people of the parish. Those previously rated included coal mines, clay, sand, clunch and gravel pits, stone quarries and brick fields. Documents show that "Headley and others" works were rated but at how much was not stated. James Jarvis and John Whitechurch had their Harlton works rated as well. Usually a horse-operated washmill was £50 and a steam operated one £100. When brickworks were rated at only £5 one can understand why there were objections by the contractors. When the rates were introduced in 1869 the coprolite contractors, merchants and even the manure manufacturers raised a storm of protest. At least fifteen appealed. Over the next few years, with the assistance of two solicitors, Messrs. Naylor and Mills, their legal objections saved them many hundreds of pounds but in January 1871 the Cambridge Sessions dismissed their appeals. This opened the way for parishes to increase their revenues from the coprolite works. (CCRO. Cambridge Session Orders 1869-1874 Headly and others - pp.71-2,124-5,142-4,201-4,252-5; Jarvis and Whitechurch - pp.97,127-8,147-8,209-11,265; Camb. Independent Press 7th January 1871 p.5; also see Cambridge Chronicle 7th January pp.8-9; Leighton Buzzard Observer,17th January 1871)

In Harlton, fields belonging to a Mrs. Hughes and Mrs. Monk were found to contain coprolites. They were valued at £280 it is likely they would have been dug. (CCRO. R57.20.C.10) In the spring of 1871, following Whitechurch's success, Christ's Hospital allowed another tenant, William Dale

> "*to did and excavate during five years 7a.3r.27p. at Harlton...(and to) raise and sell for his own use the mineral known as Coprolite...*"

(Christ's Hospital Court Minute Book Vol.18,p36)

His royalty was only £30 an acre which suggests there was a degree of nepotism involved when others like Jarvis were paying £90 per acre. Four months later Whitechurch, having finished his fifteen acres, gained a further licence from the hospital allowing him *"to dig for raise and sell coprolites from a further quantity of land on not exceeding ten acres,"* part of the Manor Farm. He paid the same £90 per acre but was allowed to work them down to eighteen instead of thirteen feet. (Christ's Hospital, Court Minute Book, Vol.18,p.88)

Clearly the profits to be made from raising the

coprolites were not lost on Rev. Thomas Preston, the Harlton vicar. He wrote to Jesus College who had given him the living of the parish, enclosing the following note and its accompanying response:-

> "I send you on the other side Dr. Travers Cross' opinion, which secures, with two other superior authorities which I have consulted, to give me the sole and unreserved right to raise the coperlites [sic] and dispose of them. Whatever however the decision maybe, I am quite prepared to expend the money for the benefit of my successors and the spiritual interests of the parishioners. I am proposing to enlarge my Vicarage House, and as the sum to be expended is not sufficient to borrow from the Bounty Office, (They will not lend less than a year's income), I was proposing to lay out a portion of the coperlite [sic] profits in this way and have my plans etc. all ready for the b/c [?] to see. Thomas Preston"
>
> 12th December 1857 Opinion Doctors Commons.
> I am of the opinion that a fossil substance in the nature of coprolite comes under the... considerations of law as a mineral substance and that the raising of such substance to the surface of the Glebe is not waste nor is the incumbent liable to account for it to his successor, but may dispose of it to his own advantage.
>   *Travers Cross.*"
>   (Jesus Coll.Mun. Livings 9. Harl. 2)

It would appear the bursar of Jesus College accepted this proposal and the glebe was dug but by whom is unknown. The profits went direct to the vicar. The next incumbent, Rev. O. Fisher, similarly benefited from the coprolites as, in June 1873, he wrote to the master of Jesus College requesting some of the money from his coprolite account to be expended on 20 perches of land. His correspondence with his solicitor, Clement Francis, confirmed that there were coprolite royalties from as early as 1868. He authorised an investment of £10 of this coprolite money. (Francis Bill Books 1868 p.402)

He did not report the glebe having been dug in his correspondence with the bishop. He ought to have been aware of the 1858 Ecclesiastical Leasing Act, introduced by the Commissioners to prevent the incumbents from profiting personally from digging the minerals beneath the glebe. Such revenues were to go straight to the Ecclesiastical Commissioners with the vicar only getting the interest from the investment. What he did write was quite revealing though as it indicated the diggings had considerably expanded.

> "The crowding in cottages is very great on account of the coprolite works. The coprolite diggers are very much influenced by one another and if one became a communicant he would be liable to persuade others." Osmund Fisher, Incumbent."
>
> (CUL.EDR.C3/25)

This was again confirmed in 1875 when the local trade directory pointed out that in Harston *"The digging of coprolites for manure gives employment to many labourers here."* (Kelly's Directory 1875)

Work was going on to the north of Hauxton in the fields west of the river and this drew the attention of two eminent Cambridge geologists, Pennings and Jukes-Brown. They were interested in a second seam which had been discovered at a far greater depth than Gilbey had first been allowed to work. (Pennings and Jukes-Brown, 1881. pp.31,35.) This new seam was of good quality in terms of its phosphate content and prompted Gilbey, by the end of

October 1869, to go into partnership with King Tuck. Mr. Tuck was another local man who advertised in the local trade directory as a "Coprolite merchant." Jesus College allowed Tuck two years in which to raise the fossils from another six acres of Impropiah Farm still farmed by Mr. Long.

The college bursar may not have been aware of the manure manufacturer's great demand for the coprolite nor how much Mr. Watson had paid. Mr. Tuck's royalty was only £100 per acre. Their lease allowed him to go down to 20 feet (6.1m.) but with a £10 reduction for each foot below sixteen. (Jesus College Mun. Harston) He had paid the college £470 for five acres by 1871 but, as the depth was greater than that stipulated in the agreement, he was allowed £75 compensation. A copy of Bidwell's sketch of their works is shown on page ... By 1871 Tuck's men had dug ten acres and, having levelled it, the surveyor indicated that the value of the farm had been enhanced by the diggings. That year, Long purchased a further ten-year lease paying a rent of thirty shillings (£1.50) an acre.

Like Gilbey, Mr. Long was known for his hospitality at harvest time. His annual horkey was held in Dove Cottage where upwards of fifty men were entertained to a dinner of beef and pudding with plenty of the farmer's home-brewed beer. In an account of these celebrations H.C. Greene, the local historian, described how some men wearing stiff straw hats balanced quart mugs on top and sang the Horkey song. The idea was to try to knock off the other's ale. (Greene, op.cit. p.17) One drinking song written at the time which adds light to the relationship between diggers and farmers can be seen below: -

COPROLITE DIGGING FOREVER
SUCCESS TO THE FOSSIL DIGGERS!

Come listen you farmers to what I do say,
We Coprolite diggers now can have fair play,
You once did us grind down, but now its our turn,
As we can get work and farm labour spurn!
We are jolly young fellows, that do not work fear,
We can work at the fossils, have a pot of good beer.
With our spade and pickaxe we've no work to seek.
We won't work for farmers for ten bob a week.
So good luck to all labourers wherever they may be,
The Coprolite diggers I mean for to say;
Success to all men that can use the spade,
He's quite as well off as a man at his trade.
Remember old farmer you once had your way,
Of crushing poor labourers and make them obey,
But now we have plenty of work for to do,
So go to the d----l and all the fine crew;
Your sons & daughters with all their fine clothes,
At the Coprolite diggers don't turn up your nose,
Remember 'twas through us you have what you've got,
But still for all that you're a covetous lot.
I've been to some works in famed Coldham's Lane,
And I've heard it repeated again and again,
That Poss will get married to red-headed Sall,
And I hope she will make him a very good pal;
There's Tifey he loves a drop of good beer,
And Hello he is not behind, never fear,
There's Pegg too he's fond of a little wee drop,
And Blinkee he keeps the swankey beer shop.
There's no harm in what I'm going to say,
But if you should meet them by night or by day,
They will ask you a question and often repeat,
Hollo! old fellow, how is your poor feet?

Where are you going on Sunday? they say,
Or anything else that comes in their way;
But still I respect them, they are hard working men,
And this is the reason I took up my pen.
So now I conclude with good luck to you all,
The lads and the men, the great and the small,
You are jolly good fellows wherever you be,
And where you got one bob, I hope you'll get three.

(Original in possession of the Sclaters, Abington Pigotts)

Messrs. Tuck and Gilbey's new undertaking and the immense profits being realised by Haslingfield Charity from the workings on their farm must have encouraged the trustees of Harston Charity. In November 1869 they received the following letter from Edward Pascoe, another interested party.

12 Cambrian Villas,
Cambridge,
November 22nd 1869

Sir,
With regard to the estate to let at Michaelmas next would you on the part of the Trust like to allow a search to be made for to ascertain the depth of fossils in the estate of 74 acres - such search to be made without causing damage to the present tenant. And if stones are to be found there I believe a customer can be found to rent the farm and also give a fair price for all ground worked for Coprolites. An answer will oblige should you have any other land that coprolites can be had from and whether you can obtain liberty to test previous to offering a price per acre for such.
I have the pleasure remaining Sir,
Yours truly,
Edwin Wm. Pascoe.

(CCRO. R59/27/2/3)

There was no evidence of a reply but one would have imagined a search would have led to the fossils being raised. There are reports of workings continuing into the 1870s with a pit being opened up in a narrow lane in the village itself. According to the contributors to the Cambridge Village Book it was worked by an influx of fifty-five migrant labourers. (Cambridge Village Book (1989), p.83.) Who was responsible is not documented.

Over a year later demand by manure manufacturers for the fossils had so increased that contractors were willing to pay much higher royalties to get access to large deposits. The committee decided to threaten Lunnis with legal action to remove him and advertised both the farm and coprolites.

Haslingfield Charity Farm
To be let. At Michaelmas next the above farm containing 74a.2r.0p. with or without the privilidge of raising the coprolite. Applications to be made by letter only and addressed to the Secretary of Haslingfield's Charities, Mr. N. Wallis.

(CCRO. R59/27/1/2.)

When the tenders came in all the offers were higher than Jarvis' initial £120 which caused him to raise his bid, first to £130 and then to £140 but as the list of main tenders shows below, there was considerable interest in the farm.

23/11/69 James Jarrod, Cambridge £150 per acre.
29/11/69 King Tuck, Harston 50/- rent per acre and £130 per acre for coprolite .
18/12/69 Prior Paine, Hardwicke £150 per acre.
22/12/69 Jonathan Chivers, Cottenham £2.5.0 per acre

plus an arrangement on coprolites .
29/12/69 Robert Mason, Reach £135 per acre but only for 30 acres .
30/12/69 Robert Clark, Grantchester £185 without, £170 with and to dig up to 14 feet.
31/12/69 J. Nesbitt £130 p. acre
1/01/70 J. Jarvis, Cambridge £140 .

(Ibid.)

One other offer came from Nathaniel W. Johnson, who was working as the agent for Edward Packard, an Ipswich manure manufacturer. He wrote from Chesterton on the 30th December 1869:-

Haslingfield Charity Farm Coprolites

We do not feel inclined to make an offhand offer for the above at an exorbitant rent and royalty but should be prepared to give a good large piece for both farm and coprolites and also a fair sum for gravel stones if you do not accept any tender and would like to treat with us by private contract. I am aware that there is a very large part of the farm which would be dug to say 17 feet depth - and I have had a good deal of Experience in raising gravel and am convinced that if properly managed the latter article would bring in something very considerable.

(CCRO.R59/27/2/3)

This and the other tenders were duly considered but the trustees awarded the lease to James Ind Headly, the Cambridge iron founder, who had been involved over a decade earlier with Earl De La Warr. Whether this had any bearing on the affair cannot be determined but the records failed to reveal his tender.

The actual lease drawn up has similarly failed to emerge. The agreement must have stimulated enormous interest as to what this huge increase in revenue ought to be spent on. Revd. Clements, in a letter to the Charity Commissioners regarding the Charity, pointed out that "*it possesses some minerals estimated at between £3,000 and £4,000 which are gradually being got and turned into a capital money fund*". (Ibid.)

Although workings had been going on in the area to the north and west of Hauxton for more than a decade the first evidence was not until the 1871 census. It recorded a small rise of 27 to 289. 34-year old Shaw Askew was recorded as *"Foreman at Copperlite Mines."* He was a lodger at 17 Coats Road. 32-year old James Marking was *"Contractor at Copperlite Works"* living at 27 High Street. With a coprolite carter and *"engine driver at copperlite mines"* there were thirty-eight *"copperlite miners,"* suggesting a considerable undertaking in the immediate area. Their average age was 26.9 with the eldest 44 and the youngest 13. As only 52% were born in the parish and 8 were lodgers it suggested there had been an influx of labourers to work what was colloquially termed *"copperlite."* Interestingly there were only 28 agricultural labourers that year but even though the diggers would stop work to help in the harvest, it must have caused a problem for the farmers.

Haslingfield's population increased 14%, an additional 109 over the decade, to 871. According to the Victoria County History it was attributed to "*demand for labour in the coprolite diggings*". The industry halted the emigration of young men, which in other villages was a common phenomena in the first half of the century. (V.C.H. 'Cambs.' ii) Of the 491 males in the parish, 114 were described as agricultural labourers, just over 21% of the males. 105 were employed in at least two sets of diggings. Martin Osbourn, 52, was *"foreman of the Coprolite Pit"*, and Daniel Coxall, 35, *"foreman of the Coprolite Mine"*. It is possible that Coxall, as mentioned earlier, had been working in the area for some time as he was also involved in the Harston pits. As well as a *"fossil carter"* there were two other carters who would have had a good business carrying the fossils to the railway station. The ages of those involved ranged from sixty-two to thirteen. As 47.5% of them were lodgers who were not born in the parish, it shows that some of the villagers must have made additional income taking in these forty or so lodgers. (CCRO.1871 census; Cambridge Chronicle, 13th May 1871.)

Barrington had a dramatic 29% increase in population over the decade. There were 164 more people giving it its highest population of the 19th century at 727. It must have been linked to the prosperity brought about by the coprolite industry. It was very much a male dominated village with 407 males and 320 females. There were 150 men and boys engaged in coprolite work. This was the largest number in the entire coprolite belt after Wicken, where 169 were involved. They accounted for 50% of the 298 working men and boys and 20.6% of its entire population. They were predominantly young men in their twenties and teenagers. Perhaps to be expected, 68.3% were unmarried. The average age was 24. The eldest was 71-year old Thomas Chapman and John Chapman, probably his relative, was the youngest at 9. There were eight under 12 who must have been missing school with parental consent. However, they were there with brothers, fathers and grandfathers. As fifty-one were related to the head of household it was very much a family concern. Only 41.3% were born in the parish and with seventy-three lodgers it confirms that there had been an influx of outside labourers- into the area. Their rents must have boosted villagers' income considerably.

Harston had a 17% population increase over the decade to 917. Surprisingly, the only person described as involved was 33-year old King Tuck. He was described as a

"*Coprolite Merchant*" living on the High Street. Out of the 487 males in the parish there were about 75 agricultural labourers and 127 "labourers", any number of whom could have been fossil diggers. The Victoria County History states that "*Coprolite digging, which continued from the 1860s to the 1890s, occupied 54 men in 1871*". According to the census none of the 127 labourers were natives of Harston, and 40 came from outside Cambridgeshire. (CCRO. RG 10/1583.) The fact that 43.3% were lodgers further supports the suggestion they were the "coprolite diggers".

According to the Victoria County History, Trumpington's 17% increase in population in 1871 was attributed to *"the demand for labour in the coprolite diggings."* (VCH, 'Cambs.' Vol.8 p.261) There were 125 additional people in the parish giving a total of 841. Although forty-nine men and boys described themselves as involved in the diggings, there may have been many others who described themselves as agricultural labourers - especially if they were raising them for a farmer. Their ages ranged from two 54-year olds to a 13-year old boy. Whilst the average age was 28.3 the table below shows that the bulk of the men were in their twenties. As just over 61% of them were born in the parish there had clearly been an influx of labourers, a common phenomenon in villages with extensive operations. 23% came from other Cambridgeshire parishes and the other 16% came from outside the county, mostly from Suffolk. (CCRO. RG190/1584)

In Cambridge itself there were a hundred men and boys recorded as being involved. There were thirty-two in Chesterton and twenty-six in Cherry Hinton. Across the river in Grantchester where the diggings had been going on for twelve years the population had increased 21% over the decade to 844. The number of males increased 26% from 351 to 448, a phenomena accredited in the Victoria County History to the diggings. Records show that there were at least two local farmers and several outside contractors involved but the 1871 census described only seventeen people as engaged in the diggings. These included two coprolite foremen, thirteen coprolite labourers and two carters. None of them were born in the parish. Most came from nearby Cambridgeshire villages. What had happened to those younger diggers who were employed in 1861? Maybe they didn't describe their work as coprolite labour.

One site where there were local workings at this time was on Shelford Farm in the western corner of Little Shelford parish near the Hauxton boundary. Maybe local people were employed here. (Ag.Hist.Review.xxiv, pp.38-9) Jesus College had allowed either their tenant farmer or one of the local coprolite contractors to exploit them from the ten acres shown on the map on page .. (Jesus Coll.Mun.,Gt.Shelford 7) There were twelve engaged in the work in Little Shelford. 40-year old William Smith described himself as a *"Coprolite Merchant."* 35-year old William Fuller was the *"foreman of the coperlite works"* and there were ten other coprolite labourers. Sixteen were recorded in Great Shelford. There were three men in their twenties from Newton described as fossil diggers.

Another indication of where it was being dug in Hauxton came in the April of 1872. James Lilley, copyholder of Royston Farm, had the 10a.1r.31p field tested for coprolites. There had been diggings at the foot of the slight rise to the southwest in Harston parish and also on the fields near the river at Grantchester and Trumpington which must have made him suspect the deposit occurring on his farm. When it proved successful he wrote to the Church Commissioners who owned the land *"desirous to work the coprolite"* on four and a half acres. The Commissioners gave him the licence in July. He agreed to pay them £50 per acre, not much in those days when land nearby was going at up to £160 per acre. (Church Commissioners Files, Hauxton 46167)

This further increased the job opportunities in the area. As the digger's wages of up to twenty shillings (£1.00) a week were considerably higher than the eight to twelve shillings of the agricultural labourer, there was a tendency for the fitter men and boys to go for this work. When it is compared with the thirty shillings a week that the "navvies" got and the fifteen shillings the labourers got when the railway was laid in the 1840s one can understand the attraction of the coprolite work. There have been many suggestions that gangs of Irish labourers were involved but the census data does not confirm this. It may have been that itinerant gangs moved away before the census enumerator appeared. According to Mr Royston of Harston, in some of the surrounding villages "*the population more than doubled and local labour was supplemented by Irish workmen*". The increase in the village's population was attributed in the Victoria County History to the "*demand for labour in the coprolite diggings*". (Sawford B. notes in Baldock Museum; V.C.H. West Cambs. No.8 p.189)

The second deeper seam referred to earlier attracted the attention of Rev. Fisher, the vicar of Harlton. He had an article on it published in the 1871 Quarterly Journal of the Geological Society. In it he described its locality in

> "*a field on the south side of the road between Haslingfield and Harlton, just under the hill. The other instance of reduplication of the coprolite bed occurred in a pit about a furlong distant, north-west, from the last... about a foot or less in average thickness*".

(Fisher, Rev. O. (1871), 'The Coprolite Pits of Cambridgeshire', Q.J.G.S., pp.65-71.)

It is possible that the erosion of the last ice age removed much of the chalk deposits and exposed the Lower Greensand whilst the earlier pits were in the Upper

Greensand. It could have been the "mine" Coxall was working but, according to the local historian, Richard Grove, there were two other contractors, Samuel Fison and his brother Joseph working in this area. They were reported to have "*leased and worked mines at Haslingfield*" but no documentary evidence of this has emerged. (Grove, R. op.cit. p.47)

To the south of Harston village at the foot of Rowley's Hill there was a report of further workings in the field east of Hoffer Bridge and Manor Farm. Here numerous bones were discovered during the coprolite diggings. Whether they were human or animal was not stated. (Parker, R. (1969), 'Cam or Rhee') There was also a reference in Pennings and Jukes-Brown's 1881 geological paper to a pit just north of Manor Farm. (OS. 409503) They referred to several centres of operation in the early 1870s.

> "*The coprolite bed has been followed all round these (hills) and has been and is being extracted from all places where it is within 20 feet of the surface... Between Harston and Haslingfield the pits were open in 1871. At Haslingfield the phosphatic nodules have now been almost entirely extracted from an outlier. In the Cantelupe Farm area the depth of works averaged about 20 feet*".
>
> (Pennings and Jukes-Brown, 1881,pp.5,37)

Cantelupe Farm occupied land between Haslingfield and Grantchester. It may have been in this area or at Button End where Coxall had another coprolite pit. He was also responsible for pits in Barrington but it was in a Harston pit that the following serious accident occurred.

"**HARSTON**. *Fatal accident - On Monday last, F. Barlow, Esq. , coroner, held an inquest at the Railway Tavern,* *concerning the death of John Dockrey, 18 years of age. Deceased was engaged at Mr. Coxall's fossil pits, and on Wednesday morning, the 3rd. inst., he was borrowing soil along a plank which was placed across a pit, 16 or 17 feet deep. He slipped over this plank, and fell head foremost on to another at the bottom of the pit. The barrow fell with deceased, but not upon him. He was quickly removed home, and attended thrice a day by Mr. J. S. Smith, surgeon, but he died on Saturday. The cause of death was rupture of a blood vessel of the brain, from the fall, causing compression of the brain. There was no fracture of the head or any bone. The jury returned a verdict of Accidental Death. A correspondent writes:- "It is a matter of surprise that more accidents of this character do not occur, for some of the cuttings the men pass over by means of a narrow plank are frightful to behold, and in wet weather, or when the men have been drinking (which unfortunately is very frequent), some of their performances on the planks are a sight not soon forgotten; but nearly every week accidents happen and bones are broken, which few of the public are aware of. Most likely had there been two broad planks instead of one narrow one, this accident would not have taken place.*

(Cambridge Chronicle 13th May 1871. p5.)

Lilley did not seem to have worked the field called Gilliam's Close with any speed. Part of it had trees that had to be cut down and their roots extracted before the fossils could be raised. In January 1875 he sent the Church's solicitors, Smith and Gore, £150

"for 3 acre Coprolite diggings at Hauxton on the Manor belonging to the Ecclesiastical Commissioners and that quantity is as near as I can tell up to the first

of January last. It will not be long (I believe) before they finish the field where there are coprolites, and when they are finished I will get it measured..."

(CCRO. L70.58.b.)

Two years later he had still only worked 2a.3r.31p. and Smith and Gore wrote to him at North Hall, Royston *"If this latter is all the probable coprolite area and you are not likely to work more write us so that we may cancel the licence. If you are likely to work any more within a few years we will keep the account open."* (Ibid.)

In January 1874 the Charity Commissioners drew up a more acceptable lease with Headly for their Haslingfield property. They maintained the same terms as the original including a condition that he pay "*1/- (£0.05) for every load of gravel raised*". They also stipulated very clearly how the funds from the Charity should be spent. It was to be divided into seven parts with one seventh going to *"the maintenance and repair of the Parish Church including the Tower and the Steeple but exclusive of the Chancel"* and that any surplus would go for the care of the church clock. Four parts were to support the existing subscription for the Parochial and Infant schools and provide for their teachers and the remaining two parts were for

"fuel, clothes, bedding, medical or other needs of those in sickness or such industrious or most deserving of the parish's poor inhabitants".

(CCRO. Charity Files, Haslingfield)

At one of the meetings one suggestion was that "*money from the fund be used to renovate the church including the tower*". Others suggested the erection of new school buildings and *"various other works"* but first the trustees had to gain permission from the Charity Commissioners who deliberated for many years whilst the fund and its interest steadily accumulated. The reason for the delay was that the Commissioners' regulations in matters of this kind stipulated that no new buildings could be erected from the fund, only buildings improved.

Rev. Williams of Hauxton gave some of the parish glebe and £20 of his own money towards the £208 needed for the building and equipping of a new school. In Audrey Elliot's history of Hauxton she suggested that part of the cost was met by selling the coprolites from the glebe behind his vicarage. (Elliot, A. (1993), 'Hauxton - In Times Past', pp.22) Documentary evidence for this has not come to light.

New workings were opened during 1874-5 when another small outlier of marl and coprolite was worked on the north side of Full Brook. According to Pennings and Jukes-Brown, the fossils *"lay in hollows... the workmen stated that the seam averaged 8-12 inches in the hollow and not more than 6 inches on the ridges"*. Whether it was worked by Headly, Mason, Coxall or another contractor was not specified. (Pennings and Jukes-Brown, 1881,pp.5,37; Whitaker, W. (1921), 'Water Supply of Cambs.' Mem. Geol. Surv., London, p.75)

We can thank the archaeologist, Sir Cyril Fox, for recording details of a find at Cantelupe Farm where some very significant Iron Age relics were uncovered by the diggings. An iron sword blade, a spearhead and the point of another spear - the last found on the shoulder of a skeleton - were discovered in 1865. Nearby was a large amphora filled with burnt bones and nails. Whether this last find was uncovered during the diggings is uncertain. Cox pointed out that during the period 1872 - 1875 when the coprolites were dug north of the river an ancient burial ground was unearthed. This was North East of the village and South

East of the field road to Cantelupe Farm, beside the Farm road running from Cantelupe Farm to Haslingfield, near spot height 71 (O.S. G.R. 413530). A considerable quantity of second century Romano-British and fifth and sixth century Anglo-Saxon grave goods was recovered from the inhumations. This included brooches, wrist clasps, beads and bracelets which were considered important enough to have found their way into the British Museum, London and the Ashmolean Museum, Oxford. (Fox, C. (1927), 'Archaeology of Cambs.' pp.255-9; Grove, op.cit. p47.)

It was in 1874 when an Anglo-Saxon burial ground was unearthed during coprolite diggings on Stoney Hill. A local entrepreneur and somewhat illiterate, Frederick Pond, set himself up as a fossil collector and supplied many museums with artefacts as well. Correspondence he had with Professor Rolleston of Oxford reveals an interesting side of this work.

> Feb. 24th, 1874 "I have sent you the Antiquities mentioned in my letter to you from harston Station they was found at Haslingfield in the feald known as Stoney Hill there is a great many skelitens beene found there was some found with those Broach but they Buried them... I have bought this little thing like a watch face."

> March 26th "I have got 3 Pots found in the Same Place... one the largest is figured outside very nice ... It had a lot of Bones Been preserved in it hade a Bone Combe in it with the earth.... The other 2 had not anything in them only earth 2 of them are small." (Rolleston recorded that the bones were human, of a girl aged about 14 and with them 2 glenoid ends of scapula of a ? calf.)

> May 20th "3 urns, the smallest very nice... They was found in Stoney Hill with the skelitons and other things. I shall want 10 shillings for the urns. I have got 4 Heads 2

are Pretty good and 2 are Broaken and some Leg Bones I have got a Bullick face with the horns on it Perfect."

"Dear Sir, I have received your letter about the finding of the skeletons I am sorry I did not hear of it amounth (sic) ago as there was several found about that time but they have run the slurry over them so it is impossible to get them but I will get you some skull and leg bones as soon as there is some more found I have been and gave the men the order to get me some more as soon as they turn up I quite think there will be some as they keep finding ornaments every few days now.
Yours obediently,
Frederick Pond fossills Collector"

June 11th 2 skulls and 2 leg bones and a little broken pot were received by Rolleston.

July 13th A little urn was found very deep.

Aug. 3rd A skull and some bones were taken to Pond, and sent to Rolleston. Work stopped until after harvest.
Sept. 30th 2 more urns were received.

Oct. 16th More relics were found in the previous week "but I have not got any of them yet there is some Gentleman at Cambridge they give a long Price for them but I shall get all I can and send them to Mr Greenwell."

Oct. 28th "I have sent you 3 urns today... the Bones in the large one was in it when it was found ... Will you please let me know if you have sent those things to Canon Greenwell which I sent in your last box ...since I have got some more things for him which I have Bought since found with the skelitons one ring was on the finger bones when found those urns was found with the skelitons they broak the Heads in getting them out."

Nov. 30th One skull and a pot containing bones was sent.

Dec. 28th. Another urn, with contents. 3 of these urns in the Ashmolean Museum still contain burnt bones; and there is a quantity of material from inhumation graves - brooches of every variety, especially small-long, wrist clasps, beads, bracelets, bucket escutcheons, etc. Several of the objects are very early in date, eg. a window urn, an equal armed small-long brooch, a bronze-gilt belt plate with egg-and-tongue ornament; as also are several disc brooches in the cambridge Museum. There are also, however, some late objects, including a debased square headed brooch.

(Ashmolean Library, Oxford, Rolleston Papers; Meaney, Audrey (1964), 'Gazetteer of Early Anglo-Saxon Burial Sites', London , pp.66-7)

Fox pointed out that records of finds in Harlton in the Cambridge Museum and a brooch in the Ashmolean acquired in 1872 were probably from Haslingfield. As diggers came from nearby parishes they took artefacts home and sold them. Similarly an escutcheon from a bronze bowl and a spindle whorl, obtained by Evans in 1874, are supposed to be from Barton. As no pagan objects have been recorded for this parish it is again assumed they were from Haslingfield. In 1879, a small earthenware vessel was uncovered containing an opaque glass bead and two bronze objects of unknown origin but the location was not recorded. (PCAS. Vol. 4, 1879, Appendix 7; Cambs. Arch. 04816; Parker, R. (1969), "Cam or Rhee", p.57.)

The discovery of the second deeper seam resulted in Headly being able to work a further thirty five acres of Charity Farm. His agreement stipulated he would dig the seam down to 24 feet (7.2m.) which must have incurred extra dangers to those working at the bottom of the trench. One such incident was reported in the Cambridge Chronicle in February 1874.

"**HASLINGFIELD**. *Pit accident. - On Thursday, an inquest was held before C. W. Palmer Esq. , deputy coroner, as to the death of William Hines. The deceased who was 25 years of age and a resident of Barton, was at work in a coprolite pit, at Haslingfield, on the works of Mr. Headly, when the earth suddenly gave way and fell upon him. When extricated he was dead. Verdict "Accidental Death".*

(Cambridge Chronicle 21st February, 1874 p.5.)

One man's death was not enough to halt the diggings and works expanded across this are during this boom period. The ending of the Franco-Prussian War in 1870 brought a period of peace and prosperity which stimulated trade and business. Profits from farming and coprolite diggings led to demands for better pay and conditions. In Ashwell some diggers went on strike and won higher wages.

The 1875 Post Office Directory for Haslingfield added *that "Coprolites are dug extensively in this parish"*. (Kelly's Post Office Directory 1875) Adjacent landowners must have been encouraged to have their land dug as a new pit was reported open in 1877 owned by Charles Ling. It was in one of his pits where a second accident was reported.

"**HASLINGFIELD**. *Inquest. - Last Saturday, C. W. Palmer Esq., deputy county coroner, held an inquest at the 'Jolly Brewers', touching the death of Henry Ginn, stone digger, aged 37. Deceased worked at Mr. Chas. Ling's coprolite pits; and on Friday morning while wheeling stones, he* *suddenly fell into the pit. A witness named Lawrence, said he did not know whether the deceased stumbled or not. - George Munsey said that when deceased was taken out of the water, he appeared to be quite dead. It was about 14 feet from the top of the bank to the water. Verdict - "Accidentally Drowned".*

(Cambridge Chronicle 9th June 1877 p4, Royston Crow, 8th June 1877.)

The West Norfolk Farmers Manure Company of King's Lynn had an agreement with Headly to supply their works with coprolite. Although he may well have been supplying them with the fossils for some time, the first documentation of such was on 13th October 1875. Eighty tons were offloaded from the bargee, Mr. Dant's lighter, for which Headly was paid £212, the equivalent of 53 shillings (£2.65) a ton. Whether this was loaded at a wharf by the river or taken to the Silver Street wharf in Cambridge has not been determined. He also sent truckloads on the Great Eastern Railway, paying five shillings (£0.25) a ton freight charges to King's Lynn (Norfolk County Record Office (NCRO.) BR.189.43)

Over the twelve months period October 1875 to October 1876 he had sold just over 829 tons, realising £2,198 16s. 9d, not bad for a year's work! After a lull for the two months during the harvest when the men were able to get good wages from the farmers, Headly managed to improve his contract with the company to 54 shillings (£2.70) a ton. By August the following year he had sold them another 1,053 tons for another £2,898 14s.0d. There may well have been further sales but there was no further invoice book in the company's records. (Ibid.)

West Norfolk Farmers Manure Co. Coprolite purchases from Harston 1875 - 1877

Date	Tons Carried	Rate in /-	Sale Price in £.s.d	Mode of Transport
13/10/1875	80	53	212 0 0	Dant's lighter
29/10/1875	20	53	53 0 0	G.E.R.
6/11/1875	80	53	212 0 0	Lighter
11/1875	21	53	55 13 0	G.E.R.
26/11/1875	57	53	151 1 0	G.E.R
4/12/1875	48	53	127 4 0	G.E.R
4/12/1875	70	53	185 10 0	Lighter
11/12/1875	56	53	148 8 0	Lighter
13/ 1/1876	50	53	132 10 0	Lighter
14/ 1/1876	41.15	53	110 12 9	G.E.R.
22/ 1/1876	50	53	132 10 0	G.E.R.
29/ 1/1876	36	53	95 8 0	G.E.R.
11/ 3/1876	70	53	185 10 0	Lighter
6/ 5/1876	60	53	159 0 0	Lighter
31/ 5/1876	90	53	238 10 0	G.E.R.
7/11/1876	80	54	216 0 0	Lighter
14/11/1876	31	54	83 14 0	G.E.R.
25/11/1876	83	54	224 2 0	G.E.R.
12/1876	120	54	324 0 0	Lighter
22/ 1/1877	120	54	324 0 0	Lighter
9/ 3/1877	80	54	216 0 0	Lighter
14/ 4/1877	80	54	216 0 0	Lighter
27/ 4/1877	150	52	442 10 0	Lighter
14/ 5/1877	64	54	172 16 0	Lighter
11/ 6 1877	80	54	216 0 0	Lighter
18/ 7/1877	70	54	189 0 0	Lighter
9/ 8/1877	55	54	148 0 0	Lighter
TOTAL	1882 15		5097 10 9	

(NCRO. Ibid.)

In 1877 there was concern amongst the parish ratepayers that the *"highway rates were becoming ruinous, and without any corresponding result in the condition of the roads from such lavish expenditure"*. The expansion of the diggings had not been supported by all the community.

> *"With reference to a complaint about the opening of the ground by the side of the road to get coprolite on behalf of the Board, Mr. Wallis explained that he and Mr. Grieg thought it would be well to get the coprolite which would have realized £80 or £100, but on finding that parties in the parish objected to it, the work has been discontinued and would not be renewed".*
>
> (Royston Crow, June 29th 1877)

Why was it discontinued? In 1876 the first signs of economic difficulties arose when Headly started falling behind in his payments. The threat of *"necessary proceedings"* being taken against him rectified the situation but there were major problems ahead.

There were still deposits in Harlton in the late-1870s that could be extracted. On the death of Samuel Miller, his trustees called in Bidwell to survey his property. His correspondence suggested that the coprolites would be worth raising as they had been dug out from adjoining property belonging to Trinity College. (Trin.Coll.Mun. Box 27, Harlton deeds; CCRO. 296 B945.14) The tenant, Swann Marshall, was given notice to quit, partly because of his rent arrears of £165. The land was then auctioned, described in the sale particulars as

> *"A very attractive, compact pleasure farm containing 79a.1r.34p. of highly productive tithe-free land. Intersected by the Cambridge and Oxford Road - part on clunch subsoil - and commanding extensive views of the Cambridge and Hertfordshire Hills - and part containing coprolites."*
>
> (CCRO. 1877 296/SP51)

It realised £3,050, a lot of money for such a small area of land. It was purchased by J. Carter Jonas, a Cambridge businessman who had set up in business in 1871 and is claimed to have benefited from speculating in coprolite land. Whether it was worked immediately was doubtful given the prevailing economic situation. According to Richard Grove, Carter Jonas' wealth came

> "as a result of capital gained in buying, leasing, working and selling coprolite land all over the county. Much of the profit was derived from buying land before the boom, and speculating in its increasing value, and then selling it to another merchant at an inflated price for mining purposes. The company today is still one of the important Cambridgeshire auctioneers, estate agents and valuers, specialising in agricultural land."
>
> (Grove, R. op.cit. p.47.)

There was further evidence of the impact the work had on the social life of the neighbourhood when in 1877, a coprolite digger, Henry Ison, of Harston, was summonsed by Harriet Anderson. She was a single woman of Thriplow, who took him to court regarding his responsibility to support her illegitimate child. (Royston Crow, 27th April, 1877) This confirmed at least part of Annie Macpherson's account. Over in Barrington there were often visits by University students, professors and members of the clergy who called themselves the "Cambridge University and District Coprolite Visiting Society". Annie was probably one of its members and gradually she won over some of the coprolite diggers.

> "It was not easy for a timid woman to approach these rough characters... at first her efforts were received with sneers and scoffing. Often she would

spend hours in prayer before she could get enough courage to approach a gang of men or even say a word apart... Gradually she won a hearing and a quiet influence among them... (After a trip to a mission London she found new resources for) *a new power was soon evidenced in Annie Macpherson's work among the coprolite diggers. Clubs, coffee rooms, evening classes, prayer meetings and mission services were carried on, not only in the evenings but at the dinner times in barns if no other place was available, or in the open fields. Many Cambridge undergraduates took part. At first the speakers were always men; it was unthought of that a woman should speak publicly... Miss Ellice Hopkins, whose father was a distinguished mathematical tutor at Cambridge, came over to address the gatherings of coprolite diggers and villagers. Ere Annie Macpherson left Cambridgeshire the fossil strata had been almost worked out in that immediate neighbourhood so that only the labour of the regular population was required but the result of her efforts were far reaching. A temperate, united band of pious young men had been gathered out, full of simple earnestness each seeking to work for God according to his measure of light time and talents."*

(Birt, L. op.cit..p.14)

Arthur Austin, from Little Shelford, set up business as a lime merchant. His family were typical Victorian entrepreneurs. They were involved in windmill building, had a small iron foundry and a brewery so it was understandable he was to advertise as a coprolite merchant. He probably bought the coprolite from contractors and local farmers who were raising it themselves and arranged its sale and transport to manure manufacturers. (CCRO. 1861 census; Kelly's Post Office Directories, 1858-1900; Gaskell, E. Cambs and Hunts. Leaders, sv. Austin; Cambs. Weekly News, 16th Feb.1894; VCH.

'Cambs.', 11,p.240) He supplied the Cambridge Manure Company's Duxford works until 1875. Their records show that they were unable to secure good rates from their traditional suppliers, so on 29th January 1872 Austin agreed to deliver 300 tons to the factory at fifty-four shillings (£2.70) per ton. By 1873 he was sending forty tons a month for the increased rate of fifty-six shillings (£2.80) per ton. When the company was taken over by Mr Bird in 1876 he had received £1,133 16s.1d. (CCRO. R60/3 1872-6)

It is possible that Austin drew the attention of H. and A. Swann, brickmakers of Barnwell in Cambridge to Little Shelford as in 1875 they bought land from Caius College in the east of parish and set up limeworks and kilns. It was not recorded whether they similarly exploited the coprolites.

Lilley did not work Gilliam's Close with any speed. He claimed that part of the area included trees that had to be cut down and their roots extracted before the fossils could be raised. In January 1875 he sent the Church's solicitors, Smith and Gore, £150

> *"for 3 acre Coprolite diggings at Hauxton on the Manor belonging to the Ecclesiastical Commissioners and that quantity is as near as I can tell up to the first of January last. It will not be long (I believe) before they finish the field where there are coprolites, and when they are finished I will get it measured..."*
>
> (CCRO. L70.58.b.)

By 1877 Lilley had only worked 2a.3r.31p. Whilst he may have exhausted the seam in that field he may have been aware of the changing fortune in the industry and decided to curtail his operations. Smith and Gore, the church solicitors, wrote to him at North Hall, Royston.

> "If this latter is all the probable coprolite area and you are not likely to work more write us so that we may cancel the licence. If you are likely to work any more within a few years we will keep the account open."
>
> (CCRO. L70.58.b.)

One reason for his slow operation was the weather. There were four consecutive years of heavy rain in the second half of the 1870s that ruined crops and reduced harvests. In the summer of 1877 there was a severe electrical storm which caused lightning fires in Ashwell and Orwell. Four lambs were killed in Arrington and

> "during the heavy thunderstorm that visited this neighbourhood on Wednesday afternoon, a horse belonging to Mr Johnson, Coprolite Merchant, was killed, the tree beneath which it was standing being struck by lightning."
>
> (Royston Crow, 17th August 1877)

In Spring the following year, a Mr Morgan was charged with ill-treating a horse at the Harston coprolite works and making it work when it was ill. He was fined thirty-three shillings (£1.65), about two weeks' wages of one of his fossil diggers. This was only sixpence (£0.025) less than the fine one of the diggers in Bassingbourn was given for assaulting another labourer! (Royston Crow, 22nd Feb. 1878)

The heavy rains had caused problems by increasing pumping costs and making the work more dangerous. Workings were left open and many filled with water to produce convenient swimming pools. Where farmers were also responsible for coprolite workings they sometimes curtailed their operations and laid men off. Greene recalled that

> "They used to leave big holes which became full of water, and as there was no law compelling the owner to safeguard such places, people from time to time fell in and got drowned in the holes".
>
> (Greene, op.cit. p.22)

There was a report that in 1877 a boy called Parker was drowned in one of the flooded pits and later another man suffered a similar fate. He was discovered by a boy who rushed to the village saying there was "*a man in the Coprolite hole dead as a nit*". (Ibid. p.42) Such was the heavy rainfall that in August 1879 the "Great Flood" drowned pigs and saw lower floors of houses flooded. Furniture floated down the street. A farm in Haslingfield was struck by lightning and completely gutted with a horse being burnt to death. It was understandable why much of the coprolite work came to a halt.

The bad weather seriously affected farmers. Their economic problems were exacerbated by the then Tory government's introduction of Free Trade. This allowed entrepreneurs to capitalise on the newly developed refrigerated shipping and import vast quantities of cheap meat and grain surpluses from the American Prairies and South American Pampas into Great Britain. Home prices plummeted. Wheat prices fell to a half of what they were in the 1860s. Many farmers were forced out of business. Some were successful in arranging rent reductions of up to 30% but others were evicted. Many farms were untenanted and there was a knock on effect on local services. Trade fell and huge numbers of agricultural and other labourers were forced to accept lower wages or were laid off.

The coprolite contractors suffered too during this period. Increased rainfall made the work in the pits dangerous. In Ashwell Museum one can see the "creepers", iron grips that the diggers fastened round the sole of the boot to stop them from slipping in wet mud. Also on display are iron insteps that stopped the spade from wearing away the boots. The rain also increased pumping costs with the additional water and made it difficult to properly dry out the slurry. On top of this, newly discovered rock phosphate from Charleston, South Carolina, had started to be shipped into British ports in the early-1870s. In 1876 coprolite production was 258,150 tons. The following year it dropped to 69,006 tons whilst 170,000 tons of American phosphate was imported with a value of £500,000. These rock phosphates were very similar in nature to the East Anglian coprolites but, in typical American fashion, they were on a far greater scale and variety. The Charleston News and Courier of 1880 reported that

> "These deposits consist of nodules of phosphate of lime, thickly interspersed with the huge bones and teeth of antediluvian mammalian and marine mammoths of stupendous and gigantic proportions; the chrysonicocrisides, ichthyosauri, hadrosauri, stupendous giant baboons, prodigious mammoth gorillas, lizards 33 feet long, and other huge graminovorous and carnivorous quadrupeds; also the squaladons, phocodons, dinotherinons, and members of the ichthaurian, saurian and cetacean families, whales 500 feet long, sharks 200 feet long, briny leviathons, voracious marine vultures and other monster, rapacious denizens of the mighty deep - land and water animals lying in the same bed. These wonderful and awe-inspiring skeleton remains, styled by Professor Agassiz "the greatest cemetery in the world," constitute by far the most valuable fertiliser known to man since the exhaustion of the Peruvian guano deposits; and are an inexhaustible source of wealth to the State and people of South Carolina, and thence to the whole world."

(Charleston News and Courier, Industrial Issue, (1880))

It was a thick seam at shallow depths around the estuary mouth and the companies working it employed cheap Black labour to dig it out. It had a higher quality phosphate content than the British coprolite and even with transport costs it sold in Great Britain at much cheaper rates. Many coastal manure companies reduced their purchases of local coprolites with the result that prices dropped an average of 20% to £2.40 a ton in 1879. Some manufacturers were only paying £1.90. At those prices there was little profit. Inland companies, as shall be seen, maintained their demand but at much lower prices. This made many operations uneconomic. In many parishes pits were abandoned. In the summer months they made good swimming pools. Several other accidental drownings were reported in Barrington. Coprolite sheds were locked and plant and machinery was left to rust in the fields. Coprolite contractors asked to be allowed reductions of their leases. Some landowners agreed but others refused and forced them to continue with the terms of their agreement and forcing them into bankruptcy. Coprolite labourers joined the many other unemployed in the area. Production plummeted to only 30,500 tons in 1880. The Agricultural Depression had set in.

Manure manufacturers suffered too. With the bad weather and foreign competition farmers were not willing to buy fertilisers to grow food that they could not sell. The prices of "super" fell to as low as five pounds ten shillings (£5.50) a ton. This downward spiral in trade came full circle when the manure manufacturers stopped their purchases of the overseas phosphates. There was no market for "super". The decline in the industry's fortune was varied. Aware of the industry's changing fortune, many contractors pulled out of uneconomic ventures and concentrated in parishes where there were still seams worth exploiting. As in farming, wages were reduced which meant many of the young, single men looked for work elsewhere.

Many manure manufacturers, in intense competition with each other, lowered prices to increase their share of the market. Some reverted to an earlier practice of adulterating the superphosphate, giving the industry a bad name. It is worth noting that British farmers' reduced demand for "super" caused almost identical problems for the American suppliers as those experienced by the British coprolite contractors. The South Carolina Ministry of Agriculture described the problem in early 1880 as being

> "...a very general and widespread depression prevailing in the production of river rock. As is generally known, the great bulk of this rock is shipped to foreign countries. The short crops, and general agricultural distress which has for some years past spread over the whole of Europe, had most seriously affected the capacity of the farmer to purchase and pay for fertilisers, and consequently diminished to a very large degree the demand for the Carolina rock. Thus not only was the market lost, to a great extent, but the prices at which the rock could be sold were very greatly diminished. In consequence of this, river mining became unprofitable. A large number of the smaller companies ceased work entirely, and even the larger ones were compelled very greatly to curtail their operations and to continue with a much reduced force and at great loss."

('First Annual Report of the Commissioner of Agriculture of the State of South Carolina.' Walker, Evans & Cogswell, Charleston, (1880), pp.11-12.)

With American supplies all but halted in 1880 there was a revival in demand for coprolite, albeit at lower prices. Inland manufacturers, like Fordhams of Odsey, Birds of Duxford, Colchester and Ball of Burwell had many directors and shareholders on their boards who still had coprolite land. Joseph Nunn, the chairman of the Farmers Manure Company of Royston, had an extensive deposit on his Bassingbourn Farm. The cost of freighting in the new phosphates was high and there was a policy of wanting to ensure a continuing business for some of their customers who might otherwise have been in financial difficulties. As a result some parishes maintained their coprolite industry during this difficult period.

Those coprolite contractors with limited funds experienced difficulties when prices fell. Some went bankrupt or were bought up other contractors. Only those with enough capital or who still had good seams worth exploiting managed to survive the crisis. Headly was one of them. However, it was not easy as complaints had been made about his work. In defence he argued to the trustees that

> "...the work has altogether been a very bad one for me having to go so deep and so much ground to turn over that yielded next to nothing and the weather so bad I cannot see that I can do more than I am doing".
>
> (CCRO. Charity Files, Haslingfield)

He requested a reduction in his rent to £120. The Trustees, before accepting this, first employed Charles Bidwell, an experienced coprolite surveyor, to examine the state of the farm. In his report Bidwell stated that,

> "I have surveyed the land which has been dug and is now being dug for Coprolites and I find that Mr. Headly has not quite completed the works which he covenanted to do under the covenants of the farmer's lease, this is chiefly owing to the excessive wet seasons which we have experienced during the last 3 or 4 years which have prevented the work being carried on in a regular and continuous manner so that the contractor has not quite completed the stipulated quantity, nor entirely relevelled and restored the lands which have been dug.... Mr. Headly, by taking a fresh lease, even if on higher terms than could be obtained from a stranger, can complete his contract

which by excessive rainfall he has been prevented from carrying out".

(CCRO. Bidwell 39 pp.139,146.)

As his ten-year lease was about to expire, a new one of seven years from September 1880 was drawn up. He agreed to pay them the same £150 per annum and £155 per acre for the coprolites. This was surprisingly high since royalties elsewhere were dropping to around £100 per acre. There were obviously commercial advantages to exploiting the remaining seam as the agreement included the same £10 per acre reduction for each extra foot over sixteen feet. This meant that the deepest and better quality fossils could be raised at only £75 per acre.

Despite his works in the parish there were many people out of work during the early-1880s which produced "severe distress". The higher wages during the early 1870s had encouraged a range of new services in the parish but with the unemployment many of these disappeared. Many unemployed villagers would have had to apply for Parish Relief and some may have been sent to the workhouse. The economic decline also put a strain on the parish coffers when industrial and commercial decline reduced their income from the rates. (V.C.H. 'West Cambs.')

At a parish meeting in late February 1880 a solution was put forward,

"...in as much as the Poor's share receives no benefit from coprolite excavations... the Charity Commissioners should give annually a sum from the coprolite fund equal to the loss sustained by the reduction in rent of Charity Farm".

(CCRO. R59/27/1/2)

The Commissioners allowed £10. Dreaming of what to do

with the coprolite fund which had risen to £6,160 17s.0d. by 1878 would have been one means of escape from the problems that beset the village. Records show that this sum was made up of £2,224 19s.0d. from Headly's first lease and £3,832 8s.0d from his second. An extract from the accounts reveals the state of the fund in 1880.

In January 1880 Headly paid a further £347 11 0 for the workings from October 1878 to October 1879. This was his last documented payment. Rev. Clements made further suggestions as to how the fund could be used.

"Firstly, the rebuilding of the Schoolmaster's house - the present building being damp and inconvenient and quite unsuitable for the family of a teacher of the present day. Secondly for the rebuilding of the Classroom and also that £500 be applied for out of the same fund for the restoration of the Parish Church - a large and handsome building surrounded by a poor population and which has fallen into a state of great decay, it being of the scheme entitled to 1/7th of the entire endowment".

	£. s. d.
Towards discharging Mortgage Debt [Charity Farm]	103 10 0
Expenses re Headly's lease	25 6 3
Repairs of farm building and School premises	216 10 2
New School Building and extras	867 0 7
Towards cost of restoration of Church	300 0 0
Expense re Coprolite account	22 2 0
Total amount appropriated by the Trustees	1534 9 0
	4626 8 0
Interest	10 0 0

Remainder   4636   8 0

(CCRO. R59/27/1/2)

A £20 salary was requested for the clerk to the governors, a reduction of the school fee from two pence a week to one pence. (£0.01 - £0.005) and an exhibition fund to be set up to help those children in trades or occupations.

All Saint's church was in the process of being restored at this time. In Rev. Davis' history of Haslingfield he quoted from Rev. Conybeare who pointed out

> *"that the golden period of increased wages and population left an abiding mark on the district in the restoration of almost every one of the ancient parish churches. Certainly much was done at Haslingfield during the 1870s and the income arising from property left by William Skelman was much increased."*

(Davis, Rev. G. E. op.cit. pp.31-2; see Conybeare, E. op.cit. p259)

It was earlier mentioned that in order to make the operation more economic, men were laid off and wages were lowered. Although the Charity account books for 1880 onwards are missing, it is known that the pits continued to be worked. However, the diggers' wages dropped 30% to only twelve shillings (£0.60) a week. (V.C.H. 'W. Cambs.') This led many men to go back to agricultural work or to leave the parish to find better paid work elsewhere.

The twenty perches bought previously out of the profits of the Harlton glebe being dug were allowed to be worked in 1880. John Whitechurch paid Jesus college £120 per acre for the right as, at the time, he was still working the coprolites in the surrounding field. (Jesus College Mun. Harlton) His and Headly's work provided at least some employment for the men in the

1880s and probably helped enormously with the income coming into the area.

It was not only Gilliam's Close that was dug. A few years later there were workings recorded just east of the river by the ancient ford and also northeast of Hauxton Mill. It is possible that these involved James Marking who was advertising as a *"coprolite merchant"* in 1879. (Kelly's Post Office Directory, 1879) Maybe it was on Marking's workings that evidence of the parish's archaeology was unearthed. Between 1879 and 1880 an Iron Age settlement was discovered during the diggings (OS.432526) and quantities of pottery and a comb were found. (PCAS. report 47, 1887, CVII; PCAS, 7, 1891, p.24)

During the early 1880s parishes in this area experienced "severe distress" mainly due to the high number of people laid off by farmers and coprolite contractors. The numbers out of work put a drain on parish relief which was also suffering because of the associated industrial and commercial decline. (V.C.H. West Cambs.) At a Haslingfield parish meeting in late February 1880 a solution was put forward,

> "...in as much as the poor's share receives no benefit from coprolite excavations... the Charity Commissioners should give annually a sum from the coprolite fund equal to the loss sustained by the reduction in rent of Charity Farm".

(CCRO. R59/27/1/2)

The Commissioners allowed £10. Dreaming of what to do with the coprolite fund which had amassed to £6,160 17s.0d. by 1878 would have been one means of escape from the problems that beset the village. Records show that this sum was made up of £2,224 19s.0d. from Headley's first lease and £3,832 8s.0d from his second. An extract from the accounts shown below reveal the state of the fund in 1880.

In January 1880 Headley paid a further £347 11 0 for the workings from October 1878 to October 1879, the last documented deposit and Revd. Clements made further suggestions as to how best the fund be spent.

In nearby Barrington the Prime family, one of the large landowning families in that parish, also had farming and coprolite interests. They closed their coprolite works and Wallis was sent in to lock out the men. This led to what was described as a riot in which Wallis was attacked and thrown into a ditch. The men were initially charged with attempted murder but later it was changed to assault and the local diggers would undoubtedly have discussed the implications of this in the village beerhouses. (O'Connor, B. 'The Barrington Coprolite Industry')

At this time a new industry had been developed in Barrington. It was the manufacturer of cement to supply the huge building work that was going on in the urban centres. Such was its initial success that many landowners invested in the business, capitalising on the location of the good quality chalk marl in the area and no doubt taking on some of the experienced coprolite diggers. Not all of them met with success however. Prime's venture went bankrupt as did others. The local historian, Enid Porter, wrote that "*the banking firm of Farrow then attempted to found a cement works on the road to Haslingfield but they, too, ran into financial trouble*". (Porter, E. "The Coprolite Diggers", Cambs., Hunts., & Peterborough Life, 1971 p.43)

Headley's work provided at least some employment for the men in the 1880s and probably helped enormously with the income coming into the parish. Although there was still some work in the fossil pits, a lot of the younger men went off to find work elsewhere, so it was mostly done by men in their thirties. William Long, by this time aged 80, had retired, no doubt having benefited from of the diggings as he described himself as "*Farmer and Landowner*" and was living in Hauxton House. (Royston Crow,1st April 1887) His son, Edward, was a land agent and Surveyor, probably having gained his experience at the works on his father's fields.

The 1881 census showed that there had been a 22% decline in Hauxton's population over the decade. There were fifty-seven less than in 1871. However, there were still four local men recorded as what were then termed *"fossil diggers."* Their average age was 34.2 with the eldest 55 and the youngest 17. As none of them were born in the parish it suggests that the younger men had found alternative work elsewhere. As a decade earlier, there were only 28 agricultural labourers and 23 general labourers who could have been involved. There was only one in Great Shelford, 23-year old Albert Northrop, who lived on Church Street. One came from Newton, aged 23, who must have walked to the works in this area.

Haslingfield's population had dropped over a hundred since 1871 to 754. It was still very much male dominated. Maybe some of the women had gone into service to bring in some income for the families. There were forty-nine still involved in the industry however. 43-year old Charles Levett, living at 104 Harston Road was described as, "Farm Bailiff and Fossil Foreman". There was no indication of Headly or Levi. A lot of them lived on the Back Lane. As their average age was 31.2, a lot higher than a decade earlier, it confirmed the change to older men's work. The eldest was fifty-four and the youngest ten. He ought to have been at school. With 75.5% born locally and most of the others from surrounding parishes it was now very much local work compared to a decade earlier. Harvey Lawrence, as a *"fossil digger and pig dealer"* was the only one who indicated he had an extra occupation. As well as a fossil digger's widow, there were three older men described as, *"fossil diggers out of employ"*, including 63-year old Charles Pond who had been working twenty years earlier and was now a *"pauper"*.

Harlton experienced a smaller drop of twenty-two to 312

yet there were still twenty nine men engaged in coprolite work. The eldest was fifty-eight and the youngest sixteen. Their average age was 33 showing how it had become mainly a job for the elder section of the employed and with just over 71% born in the parish it was primarily a job for the locals. Despite five describing themselves as general labourers the "diggers" amounted to 17% of the male population compared to 22.8% involved in agricultural work. Clearly it still played a significant role in the village's economy.

A hundred and six had left Barrington, leaving a population of 621. However, of the 237 working men and boys, sixty-one less than in 1871, there were still 120 men and boys engaged in the diggings! There were also fifty-eight in Orwell including 45-year old Charles Roads who was still described as a coprolite merchant living with his wife and two children at 14 Town Green Road. Although the numbers employed in Barrington were slightly less than those employed in 1871 it was highest number in the whole of the "coprolite belt" for 1881. Their average age was a lot older, 29.4, with ages ranging from 12-year old Charles Carter to 64- year old John Fletcher. The bulk of the men were in their thirties. As 77.6% were born locally and only 11.9% born outside Cambridgeshire it was now predominantly local work. There were still eleven lodgers and, interestingly, 61.1% were unmarried. It would be interesting to find out how many of those who moved into the parish settled down and married, bringing new blood into the parish. It was still male dominated with 346 compared to 275 females.

Harston's population had decreased nearly 12% over the decade. There were 109 less people giving a total of 808. The number of males had dropped by 84. There had clearly been an exodus from the area, undoubtedly the result of the agricultural depression and closure of the pits. Although there was still some work in the fossil pits, a lot of the younger men had found work elsewhere. The work was mostly done by men in their thirties. 80-year old William Long had retired. He had benefited from of the diggings as he described himself as *"Farmer and Landowner"* living in Hauxton House. (Royston Crow,1st April 1887) His son, Edward, was a land agent and surveyor who probably gained experience at his coprolite works. 50-year old Richmond Badcock, a *"coprolite merchant"*, was living at the Post Office and Arthur Robson, 23, was the "*Time Keeper in Fossil Works*". As well as 32-year old George Speed as a "*coprolite engine driver*" there were twenty-four diggers. The eldest was 60 and the youngest 14, and a large number of them were living in Button End. Their average age was 33, quite old for a labouring gang compared with in earlier years. Four of them were boarders and, all told, 41% were born outside the parish. There were only fifty-six agricultural labourers and thirty-six general labourers who may also have been involved in the diggings. In Trumpington there was no reference to coprolite or fossil labourers. Its population had increased by almost a hundred over the decade to 940.

There was still a demand for the fossils in the 1880s but not on the scale as during the 1870s. Two local geologists, Pennings and Jukes-Brown, in an 1881 paper indicated there were workings that year southwest of Hauxton Mill Bridge and just north of it. (Pennings and Jukes-Brown, (1881), 'The Geology of Cambridgeshire', HMSO. p.31) Maybe these were Marking's workings? At one site on the left of the Hauxton Road by the entrance to Hauxton Mill the diggers uncovered a Roman cemetery. Thirty-three bodies, some pottery and coins were discovered by the diggers. (PCAS, 6, 1887,107) Evidence of Anglo-Saxon remains was also found. Small-long brooches, an applied brooch and a large knobbed pot, possibly a cinerary, were sold to the archaeological museums in Cambridge and the Ashmolean museums in Oxford. Seven skeletons were unearthed by other workings nearby which, it has been suggested, were buried there during the Black Death.

With rent reductions being accepted by many landowners and there being fewer coprolite works the rates Haslingfield parish received were reduced. The trustees agreed to take 15% off the parish assessment *"with the exception of the Tithes, Railroads, Public Houses and Coprolites"*, these being the only real source of revenue at that time. Public houses did good trade during the coprolite years. In Green's history of Harston he stated that in parishes on the "coprolite belt" the public houses attraction to the diggers was unquestionable. Their wages were a lot higher than agricultural workers so they could afford to drink. Many of them were lodgers who socialised in the pubs and at that time it was healthier to drink beer rather than water because the water supply was often contaminated from the numerous cess pits. In some workings beer was freely available on site but its cost was deducted from their wages on pay night on Fridays. Apart from The Green Man, The Pemberton Arms and The Old English Gentleman, Greene recalled how

"...in the nineteenth century there were several beerhouses, one specially started at Button End, frequented by coprolite diggers... George Willers and friend Mr Whitechurch, who owned the Fleece Inn used to treat the labourers from time to time. On special occasions he (Mr. Wilkes, the landlord of the Fleece Inn) would put a whole barrel of beer on the table and would tell the men to help themselves and this they did right joyfully. It was the days of the coprolite digging and therefore a time of plenty for many of them. Their wages had gone up from 10 shillings to 25 shillings a week. "Heifer", a local, used to eat tallow candles so the inn had no light and then enjoy the fight or little excitement and delighted in the fracas.

Some of the small inns depended almost entirely on the custom given them by the diggers. In The Fleece Inn there was "a big room which ran the whole length of the building and it was a very popular place of refreshment in the time of the coprolite diggings. Village feasts were often held in the big room followed by dancing and singing. Important coprolite diggings were almost opposite the Inn and nearby was a brickfield. The Sign of the Gate was an old beer house that used to be where Hill View cottages now stand near the church, and it flourished during the balmy days of the Coprolite diggings. It disappeared when trade became slack after the diggings were given up."

(Greene op.cit.p.26, 49.)

In December 1881 Headley made an offer to dig more coprolites in Broad Lane at £100 per acre which the trustees agreed to, proposing the money *"to go towards a deputy overseer"*. (CCRO. R59/27/5/1.) In January 1883 Rev. Clements contacted the Commissioners regarding the possible purchase of an old cottage on the southeast corner of the school site in Haslingfield. The trustees wanted it demolished to extend the school grounds. He requested their permission to purchase it pointing out that *"...there are several acres of Coprolite money yet to call in for the benefit of the Charities"*. This was agreed to but as the account books for the 1880s are missing there is no further evidence for what else the money was used for. (VCH. 'W. Cambs'; refs.C54/18860 mm:26-8. Charity Comm. files; Ed 49/500.)

There was evidence that there were diggings in other parts of the village. Parts of The Great House Farm belonging to Lord Cantelupe, Earl De La Warr and farmed by his principal tenant, William Wallis, had been dug. (Royston Crow 28th June,1889) Charles Bidwell's report in June 1884 pointed out that

> *"Many of the fields have been dug for coprolites and are not well levelled or the top soil even restored, so that the slurry pans are near the surface and the land suffers from want of drainage. This is notably the case in no. 173, 179,107, 124 and about 10 acres of no.74. The levelling of the piece of land (no.179) close to the house has never been completed and pits have been left next the moat unfinished. Unless great care is taken in preserving the*

topsoil permanent injury is often done to land by coprolite excavating and this is so in some parts of the land".
(CCRO. Bidwell 43 p.184.)

Interestingly there was land adjoining the above which was auctioned that year with two lots advertised as having "*valuable beds of coprolites*". One of them, the 13a.0r.28p. field tenanted by a Mr. Aspleb and bounded by Earl de la Warr's land, was auctioned in September. At £530 the bidding was £50 lower than its asking price. The document suggested that it was sold to the Rev. Clements, the Chairman of the Charity, but it is not known whether he arranged to have the coprolites raised. The bid for the other 6a.2r. 30p. field beside the Harston to Haslingfield Road and adjoining the glebe only reached £200 so remained unsold. Maybe the increased depth and lower prices made it less economic? (CCRO.1884 296/SP855) It appeared that interest in raising the fossils had declined with falling prices. The terms of Headley's agreement, however, stipulated that he was obliged to continue the workings until 1887 despite a decline in the market price..

By the time his lease ended he was in arrears with both his rent and coprolite royalties. He had been unable to raise all the coprolites and level all the land to the satisfaction of the trustees so they looked into the possibility of taking legal action against him. They were told that damages and rent arrears "*would leave him a pauper*". They decided to take his coprolite plant, the washmill, trucks, sheds, weighing machine, engines, horses, tools etc. and auction it. He considered it worth £400 - £500 but the trustees only valued it at £60 which of course he "*declined absolutely*". After much discussion he agreed to pay £75 for the rent arrears give them £125 and allow them the coprolite plant in part discharge for his breach of contract. The only consolation, apart from the profits that he had made from selling the coprolites over the previous seventeen years, was that the incoming tenant had to pay him for straw and manure. (CCRO.R59.27.1.3.)

By 1888 the coprolite work had all but ceased which would have intensified the unemployment problem in the parish. As a result the village populations declined. Many continued the drift to the towns to find work or overseas in answer to the numerous advertisements for temperate labourers. Those who remained were forced to work for even lower wages, dropping from nine to only six shillings (£0.45 - 0.30) a week. Those families who were unwilling or unable to leave would have had to go on parish relief. That often meant the workhouse. In May 1889 twenty to thirty Haslingfield labourers held a meeting to discuss what steps could be taken to provide allotments for them in the parish. These had been provided in other parishes and the labourers felt that Charity money could be spent on alleviating the problems of those who helped provide the Trustees with the money in the first place. (The Rural World, May 1889)

One measure taken by Rev. Fisher was to allow the remaining coprolite on his own land to be worked, presumably with a lower royalty. In some parishes on the coprolite belt philanthropic landowners allowed unemployed diggers a chance to continue the work. (O'Connor, B. (2000), 'Fossil Digging in the Fens,' Bernard O'Connor, Everton) By 1890 it appeared there had been a slight improvement in the market as Luke Griffin, who had worked in Barrington since 1863, was still advertising in Harlton as a coprolite merchant. In July 1890 he wrote to the master of Jesus College:-

12 Brunswick Place, Cambridge.
"I have just commenced raising coprolites in a field at Harlton adjoining some land belonging to your college in the tenure of Rev. Fisher. There are some coprolites on this property which might be taken out during my work being carried. If the college would sell them I

should be glad to purchase what quantity of land worth excavating or pay a royalty per ton. If you would consider my offer and let me know at your earliest convenience as it will make some difference in my present arrangement about fixing the mill for washing. Luke Griffin"
(Jesus Coll.Mun. Livings 9.Harl.2)

In order to gain the licence he was prepared to offer the undertenant, Charles Northsole, the field he was then digging. The college deferred until July the next year when their surveyor reported,

Harlton Coprolites. I have inspected the above and find that there is only a quarter of an acre for which Mr. Griffin applies for the privilidge of digging. I consider that £40 would be the full value for this privilidge with the ordinary agreement for levelling, tenant's compensation etc. It seems to be a question whether it is worthwhile to meddle with such a small piece, but you will be the best judge. There is other land adjoining belonging, I believe, to the same property which may eventually be worth digging, but this particular piece now adjoins Mr. Griffin's present coprolite works and on that account is worth more to him than anyone else and more than it will be worth to him at any future time."
(Jesus Coll.Mun. livings 9. Harl.2)

It seems likely he was given permission as £40 would have been a worthwhile return from a quarter of an acre. No evidence of the diggings continuing in Hauxton throughout the 1880s has come to light except for archaeological reports of a find in 1899. A two-horned iron axe, a key and an iron washer were with a skeleton were found in a coprolite pit about two feet deep. The axe is said by Lethbridge to be of "Christian" type. (Ca AS Comm. VII (1899) pp.24-28; Fox, (1923), 'Archaeology of Cambridgeshire,' p.259; Meaney, A.

(1964), 'Gazetteer of Anglo Saxon Burial Sites,' London p.67; Parker, R. (1969) 'Cam or Rhee,' p.57; VCH. p.315; Porter, Enid, (1973); Cambs.Arch. 04978) The area where these finds were made is shown on the earliest 25" map where almost seven acres of what look like a coprolite works can be seen with the two pumps, outbuildings and rings which were almost certainly the washmill where the coprolites were cleaned. This was run by Edward Colchester, the son of the Ipswich manure manufacturer, and can be seen on the map on page .. (Cambs.25" 1st Ed. XLVII.13)

These may have been the works where the sixteen men recorded in the 1891 census as fossil diggers were engaged. There was no mention of Marking. The population, unlike many other parishes on the coprolite belt, experienced a rise of fifty-eight to 280. Could it have been linked to the diggings? The average age of the diggers was 33.7, still relatively old with 68-year old William Bowhill the eldest and 13-year old Albert Ellis the youngest. 19-year old Ernest Colliss was a fossil carter who lived with seven other diggers at Hauxton Mills. Five lived on the Lane and the rest on the High Street. 40-year old George Warren was the only lodger. Only three were born locally, the rest coming from nearby parishes. Amongst them was 45-year old Alan Starr with his three sons 23-year old Albert, 22-year old Frederick and 19-year old Allan. (CCRO.1891 census)

There was a dramatic decline in other parishes Haslingfield's figures showed a drop of 21%. One hundred and sixty had left the village over the decade leaving 594. It has been argued that if it was not for the coprolite works, the decline would have occurred a lot earlier. (V.C.H. 'W. Cambs.') There were still seventeen coprolite diggers though. Where were they working and for whom is not certain. 49-year old George Fletcher of the Back Lane was the eldest and his 18-year old son George was the youngest. Eight lived on Barton Road, three on Back Lane, three on

Cantelupe Road, one on Vicarage Lane, one on the High Street and one at The Knap. They may have been working on Rev. Clements' 13a.0r.8p. field. There were also three in neighbouring Harston and sixteen in Hauxton. (CCRO.1891 census.)

Harlton fared a bit better. It lost twenty-four over the decade to leave 288. Yet, with Griffin's work there were still twenty-nine men engaged in the work. Their average age was 32.1. 69-year old William Whitechurch, of The Limes, was recorded as *"Farmer and Coprolite Merchant"* with his 22-year old son Sidney, as a *"coprolite carter"*. 38-year old Samuel Patman was the only *"coprolite foreman"* in the area and 63-year old William Patman was a *"coprolite engine driver"*. Only six were born outside the parish showing that it was still predominantly local men employed. There were still sixteen employed in Hauxton and three in Harston.

Barrington's population had dropped by thirty-eight over the decade to 583. As only 121 households were listed, maybe some of the older cottages had been demolished. The occupancy rate had dropped slightly to 4.8. There was still a population imbalance with 312 males and 271 females. There were considerably fewer employed in the diggings. Frederick Coote, a 62-year old widow, was described as a *"Coprolite Merchant and farmer"*. William Coote, 46, was the *"Coprolite Manager"* and there was also 35-year old William Neave and 12-year old Arthur Homint [sic]. As there were thirty-eight general labourers it may have been that they were working for the Coote brothers. Agricultural labour dominated the employment of the 175 working men and boys. There were a few employed as brickmakers' labourers but coprolite and cement works employed even less. Henry Hart was *"Manager of the Cement works"* and only six local men were recorded as employed! (CCRO. 1891 census) This decline in employment opportunities was confirmed when the Royston Crow reported on the sale of Prime's Standard Portland Cement Company in February 1891. Was it a coincidence that three months later the Cambridge Portland Cement Works opened up at Meldreth where seventy workers were taken on? The same paper reported that *"A lad named Willers, while working for Mr. Coote on his coprolite works, had the misfortune to have two or three of his fingers smashed."* (Royston Crow, 1st May, 1891, see also 25th April 1890, 20th February 1891)

Local transport costs had risen during the 1880s. Railway companies used to charge contractors and manufacturers one shillings and six (£0.06) for a ton of coprolite or rock phosphate to be taken ten miles. With the introduction of the 1888 and 1892 Railway and Canal Acts the railway companies wanted price increases of over 100%. They wanted two shillings (£0.10) per ton for the same ten miles but if it was to a large town they wanted £0.28 per ton. A deputation from the Fertiliser Manufacturers Association petitioned Parliament to keep the transport price increases down, not only for British farmers but also for the nation's manure manufacturers. Rates were increased to two shillings and six (£0.12). This led to reduced profits for the manure manufacturers, especially since the superphosphate, by this time, was selling at only fifty-five shillings (£2.75) a ton. This was more than 50% lower than during the 1870s. (Fertiliser Manufacturers Association, (FMA.) Peterborough, Railway Rates 1888-94; Commercial matters 1890-98)

A series of strikes in the London docks and gas works for better pay led to increased costs for the manure companies. There was also a coal strike in 1890 which further increased costs. Many manure manufacturers, in intense competition with each other, lowered prices to increase their share of the market. Some reverted to the early practice of adulterating the superphosphate, giving the industry a bad name. Other countries, by this time, had developed their own fertiliser industry and Norway, for example, had started exporting superphosphate to Britain. Serious company losses were incurred which led eventually to mergers between manure companies. The local trade directories confirm the industry's demise. When the industry was at its peak in 1876 there were twenty three individual manure manufacturers, raisers and agents. There were only five in 1892. (Druce, D. (1881), 'Report on Cambs.' Royal Comm. of Agric. p.365; Kelly's Post Office Directories, 1876,1892; O'Connor, B. (1999), 'The Dinosaurs on Bassingbourn Fen', Bernard O'Connor, Everton)

In 1889 Algerian phosphates started to be imported and these reached their peak in 1894. All these factors reduced prices for coprolites. When it was so low that it was no longer economic to extract the remaining deposits, Edward Colchester, who was running the coprolite works north of Hauxton Mill, expanded into brick making. He ran his father's Burwell manure works as well as pits in Abington Pigotts and Bassingbourn. In 1886 he took on some of Jesus College's land about 500 metres east of Hauxton Mill on which he built a brick kiln. The expansion of house building, particularly in Cambridge, prompted considerable expansion of the construction industry. In 1890, he added a cement works on the site to exploit the chalk marl, a valuable raw material in its manufacture. (Grove, R. op.cit. p.47; VCH. 'Cambs'. vol. 8, p.216) Documents in possession of Jesus College show that this "coprolite land" was being rented, albeit very cheaply, from 1886 to 1900 at rents of only £20 in the 1880', rising to £60 in 1891 and £57 by 1900. What was noticeable was the regularity of rent reductions ranging from 7.5% in 1888 to 40% in 1895. Clearly times were quite difficult for agriculturalists in this area at the end of the century and branching into industrial activity would have brought in alternative income and provided more regular employment than on the land. (Jesus College Audit Analysis.)

Colchester was reported as still having coprolite workings in Hauxton that closed in 1902. That year *"the only remaining* coprolite workings in Great Britain were at Harlton, Cambridge, Horningsea and Hauxton, villages in the Cambridge area. The quantity raised amounted to only 86 tons and this was valued at £119." (Kelly's Post Office Directory 1902; Kelly's Directory of Cambridge, 1912) It is possible he was still supplying the family firm but without making as much profit. There had been a number of cases of philanthropy with landowners allowing the remaining coprolites to be dug at lower royalties or, in some cases, for nothing. This helped alleviate the unemployment situation and helped reduce out-migration.

The coprolite industry had all but ceased at the turn of the century. The last record of any workings was in 1904, by which time the fertiliser industry obtained rock phosphate from the United States, Canada, Norway and North Africa. During the First World War, more than thirty years after the workings had ceased in the village, these overseas supplies were being threatened by attacks on merchant shipping by the German navy. A government agency, the Ministry of Munitions, was established to take control of all raw materials. It was very conscious of the impact this would have not only on the country's fertiliser supplies but also, more worryingly, on the manufacture of sulphuric acid. This was needed in the munitions factories of the Midlands. Two members of the Fertiliser Manufacturers Association were commissioned to question

> "...whether the possible cause of the abandonment of the use of the native source of phosphate was not due to foreign mineral phosphate having been obtainable at lower prices rather than by reason of the beds of coprolites becoming exhausted."
>
> (FMA. Peterborough, Annual Report. (1916-17), p.76

Given the urgency of the situation it was not long before

they reported that the centre of the coprolite industry

> "was practically the city of Cambridge itself, most of the colleges today standing upon beds of Coprolites within a few feet of the surface. Within a radius of about five miles the yield was about 300 - 350 tons per acre. Further out, say from 5 to 10 - 13 miles, the deposits yielded about 200 - 250 tons per acre and the veins were thinner and usually at a greater depth... Undoubtedly considerable quantities of Coprolites have been won during the 45 years or so in which the industry has flourished... but it is the opinion of the few practical men now remaining who were connected with the industry that the cream was all worked out prior to 1885 and during the later years the "blocks" of Coprolites were in smaller areas, had to be worked at greater depths, say from 15 to 20 feet and the veins were much thinner. Mr. E.C. Colchester, of Great Shelford, Cambs., who is recognised as the best authority, having had actual practical experience in raising Coprolites from between 2,000 to 3,000 acres in Cambridgeshire, Bedford, Bucks., Suffolk and even Norfolk, during the 25 years, 1871 to 1896, when he ceased operation, is of the opinion that... To his knowledge there is only one small area of about 18 to 20 acres near to Cambridge that has not been dug at all, for the simple reason that the owner wanted such an exorbitant sum for the right to dig, even in the palmy days, that no one would pay the price and the Coprolites have remained undisturbed."

(Ibid. Appendix. pp.xi-xv)

Their report pointed out that Colchester reckoned that there were only one or two possible sites worth exploiting and from these he estimated that only 9,000 to 12,000 tons could be obtained over a period of five or six years. Edward Packard, the son of the Edward Packard who had purchased the Trumpington coprolites, felt that this was an outside estimate but agreed that there was the problem that, *"nearly all the old workmen employed by his firm have either passed away or gone away and all records have been lost or destroyed."* (Ibid.)

As a result a special commission was set up which wrote to the major landowners in the area, including the Cambridge Colleges. The bursar of Gonville and Caius College revealed that there was *"a good vein of coprolites"* in the 22-acre field at the southeast corner of Hills Road and Queen Edith's Way. This was diagonally opposite the field Alfred Jones had worked on Trinity land in 1880-81. This suggests that the College had earlier had their fields surveyed but found the coprolites too deep to be worked. (Gonville and Caius College archives, Bursary: Letter Book, 6th June 1917)

Official papers reveal that the commission managed to persuade Mr. C. E. Foster, the owner of Anstey Hall in Trumpington, to have his land tested. There was no indication as to what form of compensation was offered but Rev. De Courcey-Ireland of Abington Pigotts was offered between £30 and £40 per acre for his remaining deposits.

> *"Coprolite Deposits in Cambridgeshire. - Owing to the urgent requirements of phosphate of lime, the examination of certain areas in Cambridge and Norfolk was undertaken by the Department with satisfactory results. The coprolites occur in the form of small rounded nodules in a seam about 12" thick (0.30m.), and in the case of the Cambridgeshire deposits at an average depths of 17' 6" (5.38m.) from the surface. For their recovery, the overburden, consisting of chalk marl, has to be removed, and the raw material, after being washed, is reduced by grinding to an extremely fine powder, and is then converted by treatment with sulphuric acid into soluble superphosphate, a valuable fertiliser. As will be seen by reference to Part I of this report considerable areas in the Cambridgeshire district have been worked in former years for coprolites, and after permission*

from land owners had been given, experimental boring by engineers of this Department indicated that about 350 tons of coprolites, containing from 56 to 58 per cent. phosphate of lime, can be recovered per acre of gerund. 706 acres of land were speedily tested, and estimated to contain 242,400 tons of coprolites at an average depth of 17'6" from surface over the whole area. The recovery of the coprolites is expected to begin next month upon 114 acres of land owned by Mr. C.E Foster, which is expected to yield 40,000 tons of 58 per cent. tribasic calcium phosphate. Though the recovery of the material would not be likely to pay under normal conditions when the value is about, or under, 50s. per ton (£2.50), the present price, great demand, and difficulties of importation fully justify the revival of this industry on a large scale. The cost of winning the coprolites, including washing, dressing, and delivery to railway is estimated at about £2 10s.9d. per ton (£2.54) recovered. (Since this estimate was made a considerable rise in wages has taken place.) Difficulty has been experienced in obtaining necessary materials and machinery for the removal of the overburden, washing and delivery of the product, but it is expected that a steady production of about 6,000 tons monthly will be maintained when the plant is fully at work."

(PRO. Kew, Mun.4.6330 pp.23,37)

As well as those on Mr Foster's Anstey Hall estate their tests located deposit in fields between Cantelupe Farm and Manor Farm in Grantchester where Lilley's diggings ceased in the 1880's as well as fields further southeast behind Riversdale, down towards Byron's Pool and Bourn Brook. The Ministry gave the contract to extract the Trumpington deposit to Messrs William Muirhead MacDonald Wilson & Co. Ltd and Henry Boot and Sons. The latter set up an office in the empty shop next to what was then "The Rose and Crown". This was later changed to "The Rupert Brooke." (George Rogers, The Parish Magazine, October 1983) Unfortunately, none of the company records have come to light but thanks to Henry Boot and Co. photographic evidence has survived. This can be seen on pages ...

What became known as the "Hauxton Road Coprolite Works" got underway in the October of 1917. The main centre of operations was in the fields between the river and the Hauxton Road, south of Anstey Hall Farm, down towards Hauxton where Colchester's workings closed in 1902. (Kelly's Post Office Directory 1902) Other work started in Grantchester between Manor Farm and Cantelupe Farm. About ten large elm trees which lined the road from Manor Farm to where it met the footpath to Burnt Close were cut down. Others were removed around Tartar's Well.

A small mineral line with its own sidings was laid from the Cambridge and Bletchley branch of the London & Northwest Railway parallel to Lingey Fen and across the steel bridge over the brook. Messrs. Chivers had this constructed several years previously to allow quicker access of their produce from Cantelupe Farm to their Histon jam factory. From the bridge the line divided, one going across Tartar's Well field to the edge of the field near what was then called "Field Cottage" but is now "Old Ellwoods," and then back down to the site of what was called the "Washing Station," near the footpath. The other went to an engine shed, garages and workshops near the farm road. Three hundred yards of 24-inch gauge tramways were laid down and four standard gauge locomotives were used for the main line siding work. Two small steam engines, named the "Grantchester" and the "Easingwold", were used for the site work. (Fisher, C. (1993), 'Industrial Locomotives of East Anglia', I.R.S. pp.220, 207-8)

Two enormous steam-powered excavators, known as "Lubeckers," with an endless chain of buckets, had to be assembled near Tartar's Well. They operated on two sets of lines that ran alongside the branch line so that they could dump the material into the waiting trucks. They were used to remove at least twenty feet of top and subsoil. According to Mr

Rogers of Grantchester, they were German machines that had been used to dig the Panama Canal. If any of the older coprolite diggers had watched the operation, they would probably have wished they were available earlier. They were driven by steam engines that were counterbalanced by the chain of buckets and were roofed in to look, according to Mr Rogers, like "houses with tunnels through the centre." (Rogers, G. 'The Parish Magazine' (Grantchester), Oct.1983)

Living accommodation was provided in the form of huts near the road in Tartar's Well field and the footpath over Burnt Close was diverted round the western edge of the field to allow the whole field to be worked. The prospect of having land worked for these fossils "for the good of the country" was not enthusiastically supported by all landowners. Rev. De Courcey-Ireland from Abington Pigotts, worried the remaining coprolite was to be extracted from his estate, thanked his land agent for helping to deter the Ministry and added

"We are very pleased you succeeded in your interview and have at all events delayed, if not prevented the operations at Abington. We hear of some erections and accommodation for 4,000 men near Cambridge for coprolite digging."

(Correspondence at Abington Pigotts Manor, Sept.2nd 1917)

Few local men were employed as most of them were in the forces over in Germany and the farmers had had to rely on women and children to get all their farm work done. Whilst some University students were taken on, most of the labour force, according to Mr Rogers, was

"brought in by bus from Cambridge. Many were Irish labourers and their buses were covered in anti-British slogans. They were said to have been imported from Ireland as Government policy after the 1916 Rebellion."

(Rogers, G. The Parish Magazine, Oct.1983)

Over the next ten months, with the objective of raising almost the entire production of the 1870s in just one year, a massive operation got under way. A large proportion of the coprolite digging had to be done by manual labour. They had to shovel it into twenty-six Jubilee tip wagons. Steam driven shovels, pile drivers and railway cranes were also employed. Sand and gravel found in Burnt Close was loaded into tipping trucks and used in making the concrete structures of the washing station and two embankments. The laden, low-sided coprolite trucks were hauled up an embankment and emptied into several cylindrical washers powered by an electric generator. The water was pumped from Bourn Brook and stored in raised tanks. Rather than running the dirty water or slurry straight into the brook it ran in an open concrete channel to huge settling pans. These can be seen in the photographs. Any sediment was allowed to settle before the water drained away. The clean fossils were loaded onto waiting trucks in a cutting beside the embankment ready to be taken back to the Cantelupe sidings and then on to munitions factories in Wolverhampton. Local gossip has it that not even one ton of coprolite reached the Midlands before the Armistice was signed in November 1918.

The expense of the operation was excessive compared to the 19th century diggings. Over £77,000 was spent on the Hauxton Road Works with 60.5% going on construction and equipment, 32.4% for materials and stores with wages amounting to only 4.1%. This amounted to only £70 per week! Although the final demand for £3,000 came in July of 1918 the balance of the concern amounted to only £400. How much coprolite was raised is unknown. The contractors did exceptionally well out of it. Such massive outlay for so little a return can only be seen as the Ministry's contribution to the local economy!

As in the 19th century diggings the First World War workings uncovered yet more evidence of early occupation in this area. Much field evidence on the river gravels to the north and south of the village was systematically destroyed. The only recorded finds were when student volunteers discovered some Neolithic remains. Sir Cyril Fox found Iron Age relics of "great significance" and a Roman wharf was located in the gravel by the river (GR. 43225424). Ten copper coins and Romano-British potsherds were also found on the opposite side of the river at Cantelupe Farm. (Porter, Enid. 'Coprolites in Cambridge', CSIA Newsletter Vol.5.No.7, 1973, pp.5-6; Grove, R. op.cit.p.47; Cambs. Arch. 04929)

The sale particulars of the Grantchester and Trumpington works when they were put up for auction on November 25th to 27th 1919, show the scale of the operation. They can be seen on page .., (CCRO. 515/SP577) The sidings were lifted and the plant removed. Buildings were demolished and the concrete structures blown up. Mr. Rogers suggested that the open concrete channel back to Bourn Brook might have been buried. The river was re-cut, the fields were levelled and allowed to revert to pasture. When the Plant Breeding Institute took over the Anstey Estate the land was restored to agricultural use.

Today there is hardly any surface evidence that this intriguing industry ever took place in Hauxton. A number of long, water-filled trenches running parallel to the river can still be seen. These were the settling pans or slurry pits. They were cleared out and stocked with fish. Aerial photographs show the lines of trenches in some fields but much of the coprolite land has been ploughed over this century. A few concrete structures on the Trumpington side of the river still remain as evidence of the works. The two long low spoil tips which were evident until the 1970s as the loading banks of the wash station were considered by some to be the only real industrial blot on the County. (Grove, R. op.cit. p.42) As an obstacle to ploughing they were partly levelled during the Second World War, reportedly by Italian prisoners of war. The rest was done during the construction of the M11 and the soil was used to fill the railway cutting by the west side of the road bridge and in the motorway construction. (Liddle, A. Cynthia 'Memories', Camb. Loc. Hist. Coun. Bull. no.20, 1964, pp.23-4.)

Over the fifty or so years of the industry the landowners, tenant farmers and the coprolite contractors' business stimulated other trades. Local carpenters gained useful work in the erection and repair coprolite sheds, making coprolite trucks and cutting timber for planks and supports. Blacksmiths would have had work making and repairing tools and shoeing horses. Surveyors, solicitors and auctioneers made good business out of the arrangements between landowners and contractors. Bankers would have profited from the loans made to speculators in the industry. Brewers, shopkeepers and other traders would have benefited from the increased spending power generated by the industry. Carters would have made a good trade taking coprolites to the mills and stations. Iron works were established in Cambridge and Bassingbourn where much of the coprolite plant and machinery was made. Cottages were constructed, churches were built or renovated and much housing improvement was done during this period. What was done with the money realised by the diggers is not known. Purchasing land, building houses and renovating property was common but probably a lot would have been spent on food, clothes and drink. (Corresp. J. McNeice, Melbourn re. old builder's account books)

This unusual short-lived industry played an important part in the social, religious and economic life of this quiet village. The farmers, coprolite diggers, contractors and merchants made a good living from it and it must have had brought significant economic stimuli to the parish. It benefited the churches and delayed what might otherwise have been a greater out migration of the village's economically active citizens. It stimulated beer sales and undoubtedly had an effect on most aspects of village life, not just in Hauxton but in many of the nearby parishes.

www.ingramcontent.com/pod-product-compliance
Lightning Source LLC
Chambersburg PA
CBHW071703040426
42446CB00011B/1896